THE TRIAL OF RUTH ELLIS

CELEBRATED TRIALS SERIES

GENERAL EDITOR: JONATHAN GOODMAN

published

The Trial of Ian Brady and Myra Hindley

in preparation

The Archer-Shee Case

The Trial of Graham Young

CELEBRATED TRIALS

THE TRIAL OF RUTH ELLIS

With an Introduction
and Edited by

JONATHAN GOODMAN
and PATRICK PRINGLE

DAVID & CHARLES
NEWTON ABBOT

0 7153 6421 9

Set in eleven on twelve point Imprint
and printed in Great Britain
by Latimer Trend & Company Ltd Plymouth
for David & Charles (Holdings) Limited
South Devon House Newton Abbot Devon

This book is dedicated
by one of its editors to
Professor Sir Leon Radzinowicz
and by its other editor to
Hector Munro

CONTENTS

ILLUSTRATIONS

Plates

In text

EDITORS' NOTE

Despite an intensive search both by ourselves and by members of the staff of the Director of Public Prosecutions, we were unable to trace a complete transcript of the trial of Ruth Ellis. Therefore, the account in this book is compiled from unofficial as well as official sources.

We wish to express our gratitude to the late Eric Tyler, formerly of 'C' Department, Scotland Yard, who provided much of the information regarding the police investigations which appears in the Introduction.

We also wish to thank, among others:

Mrs Marie-Thérèse Harris; Mr and Mrs Granville Neilson; Mrs Gladys Yule; the son of Mrs Ruth Ellis.

Victor Mishcon; Hector Munro; Sir Peter Rawlinson, QC, MP; Sir Sebag Shaw; Leon Simmons.

The late J. Milner-Helme; Professor Keith Simpson; Dr F. E. D. Griffiths.

Lord Greenwood of Rossendale; George Rogers, CBE; Lord Shinwell of Easington; Anthony Wedgwood Benn, MP.

Robert Broeder; George Burnett; Robert F. Hussey; Arthur Koestler; Dennis Wheatley; Richard Whittington-Egan.

Laurie Manifold, Assistant Editor of the *Sunday People*.

Ruth Ellis's last letter, the property of Leon Simmons, is reproduced by permission of the *Sunday People*; the post-mortem report is reproduced by permission of the late J. Milner-Helme, HM Coroner for the City of London, 1940–66; the map of part of Hampstead, copyright Geographia Ltd, is based upon the Ordnance Survey map with the sanction of the Controller of HM Stationery Office (Crown copyright reserved).

The article by 'Cassandra' is reprinted by permission of the *Daily Mirror*; the article 'The Death Penalty' by permission of *The Lancet*, and the capital-punishment survey table by permission of Mass-Observation (UK) Ltd.

INTRODUCTION

Nothing has a longer preparation than the impulsive act.
Fredric Wertham, MD

Ruth Ellis was the fifteenth, and last, woman hanged in England in the twentieth century. She was also, with the possible exception of Edith Thompson, the unluckiest.

Unlike most of her predecessors to the gallows, she had not killed either by using poison or for gain. If the judge had allowed her defence to be put to the jury, she might well have been found guilty only of manslaughter. Under the Homicide Act that was passed less than two years after her execution, she would have been able to plead 'diminished responsibility', and her punishment would most probably have been a short term of imprisonment. Crown counsel at the trial hinted that there were grounds for a reprieve in the evidence heard at the Old Bailey—and had the whole truth come out, a reprieve could hardly have been refused.

'She was unlucky all the way along the line,' recalls one of the barristers who defended her. But Ruth Ellis herself did not think so. She never wavered from her belief that she deserved to be hanged.

In the opinion of one of the senior police officers involved in the case, her troubles stemmed from the fact that 'she was born humble and tried to rise above her station in life'. Actually, at the time of her birth, her family was quite well off. But her father, a professional musician, was soon to be a victim of new inventions and a change in public taste; he played the cello first on Atlantic liners, then in theatres and cinemas, and finally, with the advent of talking pictures, in the street.

He was a Mancunian, but Ruth was born at Rhyl, in North Wales, because her brother Granville had caught 'sleepy sickness' (*encephalitis lethargica*) in an epidemic in the early 1920s, and the doctor had advised a move to the seaside. She was born on 9 October 1926, and registered as Ruth Neilson, Neilson being her father's professional name; his real name was Arthur Hornby. Her mother was a Belgian who had come to England as a refugee during World War I. There were four boys and three girls in the family, and in 1933, when Arthur Neilson's musical career finally petered out, they went through a spell of poverty. It has been laid against Ruth that she did not like this; there is no evidence that it pleased the other six.

The lean period ended when their father got a job as a telephonist and hall porter in a mental hospital at Basingstoke, in Hampshire. Ruth completed her education at Fairfields Senior Girls' School and started work at fourteen as a waitress. Her father became a chauffeur, and the family moved to Southwark, in London, just before the Blitz. When they were bombed out, Ruth helped to drag her father from under the rubble and was praised for her bravery. Arthur Neilson was permanently disabled and unable to do very much work. Ruth's brothers were in the forces: one was killed in action; another, Granville, lost the sight of an eye and was taken prisoner. Ruth went into a factory as a machine minder. Then she spent two months in hospital with rheumatic fever, and was discharged with the agreeable advice that dancing would do her good.

She was now nearly sixteen. Her fair hair was darkening, but she had learnt to lighten it again; she was very nearsighted but refused to wear spectacles. In short, she had the normal vanity of a girl of her age with a good figure and a pretty face. She did not return to the factory but took a course at a small drama school in Richmond. For a brief time she sang with a dance band. Then she took a job as a photographer's assistant at the Lyceum dance-hall in the Strand. It was there that she met a young French-Canadian soldier called Clare. She fell in love with him, and he, it seems, with her.

Ruth introduced him to her parents, who were now living in Brixton, and they approved of the young man, who was a Roman Catholic like themselves. When Ruth became pregnant, Clare proposed an immediate wedding; but Ruth's mother checked with his commanding officer and learnt that he had a wife in

Canada. Though he wanted to obtain a divorce, Mrs Neilson, a stronger Catholic, stopped him. Ruth never quite forgave her mother or her church until she was awaiting execution.

A baby boy, whom she named Clare Andria Neilson, was born on 15 September 1944. The child's father sent Ruth a bunch of flowers on the day he sailed home, and this was the last she heard from him. She began to call her son Andria, and informed people that his father had been an American Air Force pilot who was killed in action; she may have come to believe the lie, for she told it to the police after her arrest.

To support her child and herself, Ruth got a job as a photographer's model at the Camera Club, where she was paid a pound an hour for work that included posing in the nude. When she was nineteen a man named Morris Conley or Connelly engaged her as a hostess at a night club in Mayfair.

Ten years later, Conley was named in *The People* as 'Britain's biggest vice boss', and six years after that he was fined £100 for keeping a brothel in Paddington. This does not mean that Ruth was a prostitute when she worked for him; both the police and the licensing authority were satisfied that the Court Club in Duke Street was a reputable place. Each of the seven hostesses was paid £5 a week plus a commission of 10 per cent on all the food and drink she could persuade customers to buy. The girls worked an eight-hour day, from 3 pm to 11 pm.

Ruth found that she could earn up to £20 a week merely by sitting on a bar stool and hiding her boredom. She did this for four years, but without saving a penny. Ruth and Andria were still living with her parents at Brixton, and these were good years for the Neilsons. They ended when Ruth married one of the club's customers.

George Ellis was a dentist; more to the point of this story, he was an alcoholic with a tendency towards violence. His first wife had recently divorced him for cruelty. After a brief but hectic courtship, Ruth accepted his proposal but refused a honeymoon; instead, at her insistence, Ellis entered a mental hospital for treatment on the day after the wedding.

He came out after two months, and the couple set up house near Southampton. For a few weeks everything went well. Ellis was sober and back at work; Ruth at last had her own home and was living with her son. During this brief happy period another child was conceived. But before Ruth was aware of that, Ellis started drinking again.

There were violent quarrels, and several times Ruth left and went back to her parents. But she never stayed away for long. It seems probable that she loved Ellis: certainly she was possessive and jealous; she suspected him of infidelity with nurses and patients, and used to go out in hired cars to try to catch him with another woman.

Ellis was sacked, and went away for another cure. When he came out, Ruth went into hospital for the birth of their child. Again she called her baby after the father. It was a girl, Georgina. But George Ellis refused to see Ruth, although he knew that she was seriously ill after the confinement. The day after their first wedding anniversary, he applied for an order to file a petition for divorce before the end of the statutory three years of marriage. The judge refused the application, saying that the parties should try to effect a reconciliation. Ruth was willing to do this, but Ellis refused. That was the end of the marriage; but some of its sad history was to repeat itself.

Ruth was back in her parents' home at Brixton, with two children now and very little money. Her brothers and sisters helped until she was fit to work again.

She asked Morris Conley for her old job back. The Court Club, renamed Carroll's, had had its licence extended to 3 am, which was much too late for the last bus or train to Brixton, but Conley gave Ruth the use of a one-room flat in Oxford Street owned by his wife. Mrs Neilson looked after the children, and Ruth went home at weekends.

A year after Georgina's birth, Ruth was treated in Middlesex Hospital for an ectopic pregnancy, a condition in which the embryo fails to reach the uterus.

A few months later, when some of the motor-racing fraternity overflowed into Carroll's from the Steering Wheel Club, two men, destined to be her last lovers, came into Ruth Ellis's life.

Desmond Cussen—a thirty-year-old bachelor, respectable and rich, a company director with a flat in the West End—was possibly the most eligible man who ever asked Ruth to marry him.

He was not a racing driver but an enthusiastic spectator. And, unlike most of the other men in this chronicle, he was not an alcoholic or a woman-beater or even sexually promiscuous.

David Moffett Drummond Blakely, who was all three in the end, was twenty-four, also single, a daredevil racing driver, irresponsible and childish. His idea of fun was to squirt soda water at people and to put ice cubes down their necks. The son of a Scottish doctor, from whom he had recently inherited £7,000, Blakely was educated at Shrewsbury and commissioned in the army for his national service. He had an allowance from his step-father and an undemanding job in an engineering works. He lived with his mother and step-father just outside London, in the middle-class dormitory-town of Penn, Buckinghamshire.

Ruth barely noticed Cussen, and remembered Blakely only for his arrogance, her first phrase for him being 'pompous little ass'. She saw each of them at Carroll's only once before Conley offered her a well-paid job as manageress of the Little Club, a drinking establishment, 3 pm to 11 pm, on the first floor of a block in Brompton Road, Knightsbridge; in addition to a weekly salary of £15, she received commission, an entertainment allowance of £10 and a rent-free two-room flat over the club, where she lived with her children. At her trial she said that she took over in August 1953, but more probably it was after her twenty-seventh birthday, which she celebrated on 9 October with a party at Carroll's.

David Blakely was already a member of the Little Club. Ruth said later that he was the first customer she served with a drink. They wasted no time in getting acquainted, and within a fortnight he was living in her flat. On both sides the attraction was almost wholly sexual, and neither of them expected it to last. Ruth was not in love with Blakely, and he—technically, at any rate—was in love with another woman. His engagement to Linda Dawson, the daughter of a rich Huddersfield woollen manufacturer, was announced in *The Times* on 11 November; his affair with Ruth Ellis began either shortly before or very soon after, a matter of days.

Blakely slept with Ruth every night except at weekends, when he went home to Penn: a seemingly odd arrangement, as his weekday job was at Penn, but he was not a great worker and he had a busy social life. He had a flat with a separate side-entrance in a wing of his step-father's large house, The Old Park, and this was the scene of some wild parties attended by his motor-racing friends.

Ruth never saw the inside of the flat. Blakely made it plain that he did not think his mother would approve of his association with an ex-waitress. Especially, perhaps, as his father had been accused of killing one in Sheffield.

Phyllis Staton had been Dr John Blakely's mistress for two years when, in 1934, she became pregnant. He gave her the drug pituitrin. When he saw she was dying, the doctor dumped her on her parents' back doorstep and drove away in the hope that he would not be recognised. But someone saw him; not only that, but the girl, before collapsing on the kitchen floor, told her parents that the doctor had brought her. They called an ambulance which took her to hospital, where she died the next day. When Dr Blakely was arrested and charged with murder, he admitted his affair with Phyllis Staton but claimed that she had also been with other men and had picked on him because he was 'better off'; he also admitted that he had supplied the girl with an abortifacient drug, but pleaded not guilty on the ground that there was no proof that she had taken it. At the Sheffield Magistrates' Court, the prosecution put forward the theory that he had used pituitary extract because he knew that the drug could not be detected in a post-mortem examination. The magistrates, however, decided that the evidence did not constitute a *prima facie* case, and the doctor was discharged without a legal stain on his character. Six years later, his wife divorced him for adultery, and soon afterwards married a racing driver named Humphrey Cook.

At the end of 1953, only a short time after they started living together, David Blakely made Ruth Ellis pregnant. She got out of the mess, as she called it at her trial, at her own expense and, she said, after declining Blakely's offer of marriage. This offer could hardly have been sincere, as she would have to wait nearly another year for a divorce, and Blakely had still not introduced her to his mother or even admitted her existence to anyone at Penn.

She did not seem to mind this exclusion, but pressed him to

take her to a motor-race meeting. When at last he gave in, she understood his reluctance. All the friends of Blakely's she had met in drinking clubs had been men. At the race meeting she had her first encounter with their wives and fiancées, who treated her with the studied politeness they normally reserved for their charwomen. Their disapproval was not of her sexual morals, which were much the same as their own. They were just sorry to see David being dragged down by a woman who was so obviously his—and their—social inferior. Their forced civility embarrassed him more than it embarrassed Ruth, for, like them, he was a snob. According to Ruth's version of their story, he once told her that he was the social light of Buckinghamshire. If David Blakely ever despised himself, it was for falling in love with a woman beneath him. Not that he would admit to his friends that he even liked Ruth Ellis; the kindest thing he had to say of her was that she was 'good in bed'.

Among his friends and acquaintances whom Blakely introduced to the Little Club was Desmond Cussen, who almost at once became infatuated with Ruth. Alexander Engleman, the club's receptionist and artist, was to sum up the situation when the police questioned him a week before Ruth Ellis was hanged: 'David Blakely, a nice boy, was very friendly indeed with her. Desmond Cussen was trying to be friendly with her but she didn't seem to want much to do with him.' She occasionally let Cussen take her to motor-race meetings.

When Morris Conley learnt that Blakely was living with Ruth, he started to charge her rent for the flat. She did not ask Blakely to share the rent, and he did not offer anything; he was already becoming casual about paying for drinks at the bar. He chose this time to start building a new racing car, 'The Emperor', with Anthony Findlater, a friend who had studied and worked as an automobile engineer; they rented a workshop in Islington, and Blakely paid Findlater £10 a week to do most of the work. Findlater and his wife Carole were probably Blakely's best friends. They disliked Ruth, and she disliked them; her antipathy increased as she grew fonder of Blakely.

She had been at the Little Club about six months when her husband paid her a visit. He found her working environment so congenial that she had to let him sleep it off on a divan. George

Ellis was working as a schools dental officer at Warrington, Lancashire, and had come to talk about their daughter, Georgina, whom he wanted to be adopted. Eventually Ruth let him take the child back with him. On 26 May 1954 Ellis filed a petition for divorce on the grounds of mental cruelty by his wife, alleging that she had abused and nagged him and accused him of having improper relations with other women. She denied the allegations and blamed his excessive drinking for the break-up of the marriage.

Early in June, Blakely went to Le Mans to drive in the 24-hour race. On the eleventh he sent a postcard:

> Arrived OK. Haven't had a drink for 3 days!!! Wish you were here. Will see you Tuesday. Love, David.

Tuesday was the fifteenth, two days before Blakely's birthday, and Ruth planned a party for him. He did not come back in time, and Ruth surprised Cussen by telling him that he could sleep with her: 'I'm not married to David, and I can lead my own life,' she explained. For a couple of weeks Cussen was her lover. Then Blakely came back—he had been racing at Rheims—and Ruth held the belated birthday party. It was not a success. Carole Findlater was offended and left early; Blakely arrived late and was silent and morose. He did not tell Ruth where he had been until she asked him about his marriage plans. Then he said that he had broken off his engagement to Linda Dawson, and had been having a farewell drink with her in the bar of the Hyde Park Hotel.

The next three weeks may have been the happiest in Ruth Ellis's life. Blakely was, for him, considerate and attentive, and flatteringly jealous when she smiled at a customer in the club. It appeared to her at this time that she had no reason for jealousy. The illusion was soon shattered, however: one night they went to bed and, as he stretched over to switch off the light, she saw 'love bites' upon his shoulders and the back of his neck.

She insisted that he leave. Early in the morning he telephoned to say that he had spent the night in the Islington workshop and was cold and miserable and wanted to come back. She refused to let him. He arrived at the club when it opened that afternoon, but she stayed upstairs. Eventually, after again telephoning to try to make her change her mind, he walked up to the flat and begged her to forgive him. He asked her to marry him and, when she pointed out that his family would not agree and that he might lose his allowance, he said that they could marry secretly. Believing him, Ruth decided not to defend her husband's suit for divorce.

In August, Blakely went to Zandvoort to race an MG; he had wanted Ruth to go with him, but she would not leave the club. For once, he was punctual in coming back, perhaps because he was jealous of Desmond Cussen. As infatuated with Ruth as ever, Cussen continued to behave to her as a kind and considerate friend. When he heard that she wanted to send Andria to boarding school, he gave her the money for the fees. When she found it hard to pay the rent, he invited her to stay at his flat at Goodwood Court, in Devonshire Street, but this she refused because it would have meant leaving Blakely.

By now, she was virtually keeping Blakely, who was spending all his money on 'The Emperor'. He told her that his step-father had threatened to cut off his allowance, and talked of committing suicide. He was drinking very heavily: an ominous reminder of George Ellis. In October there was another reminder, when he punched her after accusing her of being too friendly with a customer at the bar. More blows followed, always with the same excuse; but always, too, when Blakely was drunk. One of the barmaids at the club, Jacqueline Dyer, a French girl married to an English medical student at St George's Hospital, saw the bruises on Ruth's body, and once saw Blakely push her out of the flat with such force that she fell downstairs.

Blakely became increasingly resentful of Ruth's friendliness to customers, and asked her to give up the club; at the same time he began telling friends that he wanted to leave her but she would not let him go. Blakely's behaviour in the club—his belligerent jealousy when drunk, his juvenile horseplay in lighter alcoholic moods—had lowered the takings, and Morris Conley complained. The upshot was that Ruth quarrelled with Conley and gave notice. She asked Cussen if she could stay in his flat until she found another job. He agreed, and she moved into Goodwood Court shortly before Christmas, telling Cussen that she did not intend to live with Blakely again.

On the evening of Christmas Day, 1954, Ruth and Cussen went to a club with Jacqueline Dyer and another friend. Blakely telephoned Ruth at the club and said that he was in Cussen's flat; Ruth's son, Andria, who was home for the school holidays, had let him in. They all went back and found Blakely very drunk. He said that he had called to give Andria a toy pistol as a Christmas present. Ruth angrily said that he had promised not to call that evening, and Cussen realised that they had spoken on the telephone earlier in the day. Blakely and Ruth quarrelled and then drove off together, with Cussen following in case Blakely had an accident.

They drove to the Findlaters' flat in Tanza Road, Hampstead. The Findlaters were away for Christmas but Blakely had a key. Cussen saw them go in and then drove home alone. The next morning, Boxing Day, Ruth returned to Goodwood Court, and Blakely went on to Brand's Hatch to drive 'The Emperor' in its first race, the Kent Cup, in which it was placed second.

During the next couple of weeks Blakely and Ruth slept together in a hotel on several occasions. Blakely had violent fits of jealousy because Ruth was living at Cussen's flat, but at the same time was telling Anthony Findlater that he wanted to break with her: 'Every time I leave her, she creates a scene and forces me back.'

In actuality, she had never yet created a scene. Blakely therefore stage-managed one for Findlater's benefit, telephoning him one evening and asking him to 'come and get me out of trouble'. Findlater drove to Goodwood Court with a mutual friend, Clive Gunnell, and they found Blakely and Ruth together. Blakely had scratches on his face, and they had evidently been fighting. 'I want to break off with her but she won't let me go,' Blakely claimed. Findlater said: 'Come on, David. Let's go,' and the three men walked out, Ruth following and making sarcastic remarks about Blakely's courage. When she got into Blakely's car the men got into Findlater's. Ruth at once got out and leaned through Findlater's window so that he could not drive away. The men got out, Gunnell keeping Ruth talking while Findlater quietly told Blakely to drive off in his own car. When Ruth saw him go she became hysterical. Findlater and Gunnell took her to a café for coffee and then drove her back to Cussen's flat.

This was a naïve but apparently successful attempt on Blakely's part to convince Findlater that he was trying to leave Ruth but could not get away: naïve, because plainly if she had been able to detain him physically, she could easily have stopped him from telephoning for help. In fact, Blakely had gone out after the fight, telephoned Findlater from a public call box, and then returned to the flat to wait to be 'rescued'.

The day after the Findlater rescue, Ruth sent a telegram to Blakely at Silicon Pistons, the engineering firm where he worked:

Charges to pay ——s.——d.
RECEIVED

POST OFFICE
TELEGRAM

No. POST
OFFICE STAMP

HIGH WYCOMBE BUCKS
10 JAN. 55

Prefix. Time handed in. Office of Origin and Service Instructions. Words.
48

At—m
From
By

1750 3.32 LANGHAM XN22

At—m

By

PERSONAL MR D AND D BLAKELEY SYLICUM PISTONS LTD
PENN-BUCKS =

HAVENT YOU GOT THE GUTS TO SAY GOODBYE TO MY FACE

= RUTH

For free repetition of doubtful words telephone "TELEGRAMS ENQUIRY" or call, with this form at office of delivery. Other enquiries should be accompanied by this form, and, if possible, the envelope. B or C

J.G.(P)Ltd.–51–4424

According to her, Blakely came back, not to say goodbye, but to tell her that he could not live without her. Again he promised marriage. He would soon have the opportunity, for George Ellis was awarded a decree nisi on 14 January 1955, and at that time the period before decrees became absolute was only six weeks.

While Cussen was away, Blakely went to the flat and made love to Ruth there; then he became furiously jealous because she was living in Cussen's flat. Once more they quarrelled and fought.

Ruth decided that she had to escape from the flat, and that the only way to do so was to get another job. Not wanting to work in clubs again, she thought she would stand a better chance of finding a decent job if she learnt French. To this end Cussen contacted the French Institute in Kensington and engaged one of their teachers, Mrs Marie-Thérèse Harris, to give Ruth private tuition, which usually took place at Goodwood Court. At least once (and it is important to remember this) a lesson was given in another man's flat.

The French tuition, which began on 17 January 1955, was a complete failure. Sometimes Ruth was not in the flat when Mrs Harris arrived; even when she was there, she was unable to concentrate, and talked rapidly and nervously about other things.

On the night of 6 February, Blakely and Ruth made love in Cussen's flat for the last time. Afterwards, in a fit of drunken jealousy, Blakely punched and kicked her, then walked out. She stayed in the flat the following day, and late at night asked Cussen to drive her to Penn. While Cussen waited in the car, she knocked at the door of Blakely's flat. Blakely dressed, talked to her, and then drove off in his own car. Cussen took Ruth back to Goodwood Court.

The next morning he saw that Ruth's body was so badly bruised she could hardly walk. He wanted to take her to hospital, but she said she had to see David first. Cussen again drove towards Penn, and on the way they saw Blakely's grey-green Vanguard parked outside the Bull Hotel at Gerrards Cross. Cussen went into the bar and pulled Blakely outside. 'Now try beating me up instead of a woman,' he shouted. Blakely declined the invitation, and Cussen called him a coward. After speaking briefly to Ruth, Blakely went back into the bar. Ruth seemed satisfied by the encounter, and Cussen drove her to the casualty department at Middlesex Hospital, where she was examined by Dr Robert Hunter Hill, who found multiple bruises on both arms and legs, the left hip, and around the left eye; there was a more severe bruise over her left ankle, but an X-ray showed no fracture. When asked the cause of the injuries, she said that she had been beaten up by a friend who was a racing driver. After treatment, Dr Hill told her to return in three days, but he never saw her again.

Back at Cussen's flat, a bunch of red carnations was delivered for Ruth, with a card saying:

Sorry' Darling, I Love You. David.

She and Blakely met again in the evening. Afterwards she told Cussen that she had to go and live in a flat of her own at once, and he agreed to pay her rent. The next day she answered an advertisement in the *Evening Standard* for a furnished one-room service flat at 44 Egerton Gardens, near Brompton Oratory in Kensington, with a rent of six guineas a week. She told the housekeeper, Mrs Winstanley, that she wanted the flat for her husband and herself, and asked for a vase because 'Mr Ellis' was very particular about having flowers around.

At about the time she was making these arrangements, Blakely was in the Bull at Gerrards Cross, telling the barman that he had finished with Ruth; yet the next day, he and Ruth moved into Egerton Gardens as Mr and Mrs Ellis.

Cussen called for her most mornings after Blakely had gone to work. He was still incurably in love with her, still asking her to marry him. Mrs Harris continued to try to teach her French in Cussen's flat for another two weeks, but then Ruth said that she would be busy for a few days and would let Mrs Harris know when she was ready to start lessons again.

Now it was Ruth's turn to be jealous. She learnt from Blakely himself that he was having an affair with a married woman in Penn; he even told her the woman's name and address. When she became angry, she received more bruises on her shoulders and another black eye.

On the evening of 24 February she yet again asked Cussen to drive her to Penn. They saw Blakely's car outside the Crown, and Cussen went into the bar to find Blakely playing darts with a party that included the married woman. Blakely left hurriedly.

Cussen and Ruth returned to London. But at six o'clock the next morning she telephoned Cussen, and he drove her back to Penn. It was like pursuing George Ellis again, except that she did not have to hire a car. Blakely's Vanguard was not in his garage, so they drove to the married woman's house and waited. At 9 am

Blakely walked out, saw Cussen's car, and ran back inside. The married woman agreed to drive him to work, but when she opened her car door for Blakely, Ruth ran across and slammed it shut. However, after a brief conversation with Blakely, Ruth let him go. She and Cussen followed him to the factory, then Ruth went back and apologised to the woman, who invited her in for coffee and said that Blakely had slept in the spare bedroom. When Ruth and Cussen met Blakely in the Crown at lunch-time, Blakely said that he had slept on the settee in the woman's living-room.

The three of them met again that evening at the British Racing Drivers Club dance at the Hyde Park Hotel. Cussen, after putting make-up on her shoulders to cover the bruises, had driven Ruth to the dance. There she proposed a toast to her divorce, which had been made absolute that day, but Blakely refused to drink with her. Cussen, persistent as ever, asked her to marry him, but she only wanted him to drive her back to Egerton Gardens.

According to her account, she found Blakely beside her in bed when she woke the next morning. Yet later that day, over lunch at the Crown, Blakely told the married woman: 'Ruth is madly in love with me, but I hate her guts.'

Mrs Harris, who remembers Ruth as 'a simple soul', did not hear from her pupil again. Instead, she herself waited until 5 March and then wrote saying that she thought it would be a waste of time to go on, and enclosing a cheque for the unearned part of the fee. On 7 March, Ruth started a three-weeks' modelling course, for which Cussen paid the fee. During the course, she learnt that she was pregnant once again.

At first, she said later, Blakely seemed pleased, and talked about 'little David'; but then his mood changed: 'I can just about afford seven shillings a week,' he said. There was no suggestion of marriage. Ruth swallowed her pride and went to talk to Carole Findlater, who had a child less than a year old. Mrs Findlater was out, so Ruth talked to Anthony Findlater instead, telling him that she and Blakely had been quarrelling again. 'It's about time you two either started living together amicably or not living together at all,' said Findlater. Ruth replied curtly that David could make it up or break it off at any time he liked.

Soon after this conversation, Blakely left Ruth again. He told Findlater that he did not believe she was pregnant and that he was not going back to her. Ruth pursued him to the garage in Rex Place, Mayfair, where he was now keeping 'The Emperor'. She asked him for his key to her flat, but he refused to give it to her. She enlisted Cussen's help to get it back, and they went to the Steering Wheel Club where, after an argument, Cussen knocked Blakely down and took the key. A few days later, when Blakely saw Ruth in the Stirrup Club and opened her handbag to look for the key, she smacked his face, and he left the bar. When she got home, she found him waiting outside. He told her that he had finished his affair at Penn, and wanted to come back to her. Weakly, Ruth assented. 'Mr Ellis' was home again at Egerton Gardens.

At lunch-time the following day, Ruth got Cussen to drive her to the Crown in Penn where, once again, she found Blakely with the married woman. Back in the flat at Egerton Gardens, they had a violent argument. According to her version, he punched her on the cheek, put one hand round her throat and punched her in the stomach with the other hand. A few days later, on 28 March, she had a miscarriage.

Blakely did not even ask her how she felt. Nevertheless, she followed him to Rex Place, where he had gone to help Findlater get 'The Emperor' ready for a race at Oundle Park.

'You'll never have any luck, the way you treat me,' she told him. 'I'll stand so much from you, David, but you can't go on walking over me for ever.'

'You'll stand it because you love me,' he replied.

Two days later, the car was ready and Blakely was pleasant again. Ruth telephoned Jacqueline Dyer to say that she was very happy because David was going to marry her. They drove together, with Findlater, to Oundle Park, and Ruth watched Blakely drive 'The Emperor' on a practice run. The engine blew up, and he had to scratch from the race. He blamed Ruth for the trouble, saying that she had 'jinxed' him. Anger quickly past, they slept together in a hotel in Chester, watched the racing the next day, and spent another night in the hotel. On Sunday, 3 April, they towed 'The Emperor' back to London.

Andria came home for his Easter holidays. Ruth, still bleeding from her miscarriage, was in bed with a chill for two days. Blakely seemed unconcerned. He stayed out late both nights, yet

KEN WOOD
Ladies Open-air Bathing Pond
St. Columba's Hospital
HAMPSTEAD HEATH
Manor Ho. Hosp. (Women)
Vale of Health
Hampstead Ponds
Whitestone Pond
Sports Grd.
Tumulus
PARLIAMENT HILL
Band Stand
Parliament Hill 319 ft.
HAMPSTEAD
Ponds
New End Hosp.
Children's Playgr.
Running Track
Athletic Grd.
Hampstead Heath
HAMPSTEAD HIGH ST.
ROSSLYN
Court Ho. Police Stn.
Soldier's Daughter's Ho.
G.P.O. Sorting Off.
GOSPEL OAK
Gospel Oak Estate
Hampstead Gen. Hosp.
Royal Free Hosp.
Belsize Park
HAVERSTOCK
Old Town Hall
St. Dominic's Priory
Almshos.
Mat. Hosp.
University College Sch.
Holly Ct. Open Air
Convent Cha.
The Eagles
Westfield
MALDEN
GRAFTON
0
¼
½ M

on Wednesday, 6 April, came home in a happy mood, and gave Ruth a new photograph of himself which he inscribed: 'To Ruth with all my love, from David.' According to her evidence at the trial, he also said that he would soon have some money, and again talked about their getting married.

The following evening, 7 April, he took her to a cinema, and afterwards they made plans for Easter. He said that he had to do something about 'The Emperor' the next day, Good Friday, but asked Ruth to go with him to Hampstead in the evening for drinks with the Findlaters. They discussed other outings for the holiday weekend, and Ruth mentioned that she had an appointment with her solicitors on the Tuesday after Easter, to clear up some points regarding Georgina's adoption.

They went to bed and made love for the last time.

When Blakely left in the morning, they were still on the best of terms; he promised to be back at eight to take her to the Findlaters'. During the afternoon, Cussen called and took Ruth and Andria to see a film. He drove her home at 7.30.

By then, Blakely was already having drinks with the Findlaters in their local pub.

The Magdala is a quiet pub at the foot of South Hill Park, a looped cul-de-sac on the edge of Hampstead Heath. This calm, almost rural piece of London looks an unlikely stage for a drama of passion, jealousy and murder. Yet, by an eerie coincidence, the last woman to be hanged in England before Ruth Ellis had, some months before, committed an equally spectacular killing in the same modest byway. Mrs Styllou Christophi, a Cypriot, strangled her daughter-in-law after fracturing her skull with an iron ashplate, then soaked the body in paraffin and set it alight in the back garden; a neighbour, alarmed by the flames, was reassured when he saw the burning corpse, for he assumed that the Cypriots were burning a tailor's dummy.

There was no clamour for a reprieve when Mrs Christophi was sentenced to death; all the sympathy was for her victim, a young German woman, the mother of three small children. Mrs Christophi was hanged ten days before Christmas 1954. This unseasonable inclemency was probably induced by a police report from Cyprus saying that, thirty years earlier, she had been acquitted of murdering her mother-in-law by ramming a flaming torch down her throat.

In the saloon bar of the Magdala, on the evening of Good Friday, 8 April 1955, David Blakely looked at his watch and told the Findlaters that he would have to go and collect Ruth. Anthony Findlater said that Blakely was foolish to continue seeing Ruth when he wanted to break off the relationship, but Blakely explained that he feared she might make another scene at Penn. Findlater invited Blakely to stay with him and his wife for the weekend, and said that he would cope with Ruth if she came along. Finally, Blakely accepted the invitation, and he and the Findlaters went back to the flat in Tanza Road.

Ruth telephoned the flat at half-past nine, but was told by Findlater that David was not there. She waited until nearly midnight, then telephoned Cussen and asked him to drive her to Tanza Road, where she saw Blakely's Vanguard parked outside No. 29, the house where the Findlaters lived. She telephoned the flat from the nearest call-box, but whoever answered recognised her voice and hung up. She went to the flat, rang the doorbell for a long time without getting an answer, then turned to Blakely's car. This was actually a converted van, with windows replacing the side panels. She began to bang on these windows. Blakely watched from his bedroom, then woke Findlater, who telephoned the Hampstead police.

When Inspector Harry Makin and other officers went to the scene, Ruth was ringing the doorbell again. Findlater came out in pyjamas and dressing gown to complain that she was disturbing the peace and damaging a car belonging to his guest. Makin saw that a rubber-embedded car window had been forced in. He asked Ruth if she had done this. 'Yes,' she replied, 'the car is just as much mine as his. I've been living with him for two years. I'll stay here until I see him. I'll pay for the damage.' Her voice was quiet and normal. Findlater said that Blakely was not going to see her, and Makin advised her to go home. When the police had left, Ruth forced in the two rear windows of the car. Findlater telephoned the police again, but by the time they came, at 2.30 am, Ruth was being driven away in Cussen's car.

At 8.30 am on 9 April, Ruth telephoned Findlater, who recognised her voice and hung up. Later he and Blakely drove to the garage in Rex Place to repair the car's windows, and there were two more calls while they were there.

In the afternoon the Findlaters took their baby out in the car; their attractive new nanny carried the child and sat with Blakely in the back. In the evening they held a party which went on until well after midnight.

At about nine o'clock on the morning of Easter Sunday, 10 April, the telephone rang and was answered by Findlater. He heard Ruth say: 'I hope you're having an enjoyable holiday . . . ' but he put the receiver down, missing the rest: ' . . . because you've ruined mine.'

The Findlaters' nanny went home after lunch. She would have taken a bus or train to Victoria Station, but Blakely volunteered to drive her there. He was away for about two hours, and explained to Findlater that he had spent an hour in a cinema on the way back. Later the Findlaters and Blakely took the baby out on Hampstead Heath.

In the evening Clive Gunnell came, and the group listened to records and drank beer. At about nine o'clock Blakely and Gunnell drove down to the Magdala to fetch more beer. Blakely parked his car with the driver's seat next to the kerb and locked the door. He was security-conscious, and had had the car fitted with explosive 'banger' caps that would go off if anyone tried to steal it.

The two men had a drink in the saloon bar and ordered three quarts of bitter to take away. At about 9.15 another customer—an off-duty policeman, Alan Thompson—noticed a blonde woman wearing spectacles peering into the bar through a rippled-glass window near the door.

Blakely and Gunnell left at about 9.20. Two youths were standing outside the tobacconist's shop next door. A bank official and his wife, Donald and Gladys Yule, were walking down Parliament Hill towards the Magdala; Mrs Yule's son by her first marriage had committed suicide on Good Friday, and she felt in need of a drink.

Gunnell walked round Blakely's car to the front passenger door and waited for Blakely to unlock it from inside. As Blakely went to the driver's door he turned slightly and saw Ruth standing on the pavement with her back to the wall of the Magdala. He ignored her and turned back to the car. A second later, she took a revolver from her handbag and fired a shot.

Blakely ran for cover, ducking round the back of the car; he might have been quicker if he had not drunk four pints of beer that evening. Ruth fired again. For a moment, Gunnell thought the explosions were the theft-warning 'bangers' until he saw Blakely running round the car with Ruth after him.

Blakely reached the pavement and collapsed face down. Ruth stood over him and fired until the revolver was empty. After the sixth shot, one of the youths heard two or three distinct clicks of the empty gun's hammer. One of the last shots ricocheted off the pavement and hit Mrs Yule in the hand.

Gunnell knelt by his friend for a moment, then stood up. Ruth told him to call the police, and he ran back into the saloon bar shouting for assistance.

PC Alan Thompson was already in the street. Blakely lay moaning and bleeding from the mouth. Ruth stood with her back to the wall again, the revolver still in her hand. She told Thompson to telephone the police. 'I *am* the police,' he said as he took the gun. There seemed no need to preserve the fingerprints, but Ruth Ellis might be alive today if he had done so. Thompson said that he was going to detain her. He cautioned her with the usual formula, to which she made no reply. A few minutes later an ambulance arrived to take Blakely to New End Hospital, where he was found to be already dead. Thompson took Ruth Ellis to Hampstead Police Station.

At 11.30 pm, an hour and a half after her arrival at the station, she was interviewed by three CID officers, Detective Superintendent Leonard Crawford, Detective Chief Inspector Leslie Davies, and Detective Inspector Peter Gill, all of 'S' Division, of which Hampstead is a part.

'I have seen the dead body of David Blakely at Hampstead Mortuary,' Crawford said to her. 'I understand you know something about it.' He then cautioned her, as he had cautioned Mrs Styllou Christophi in the same station nine months before. Through an interpreter, Mrs Christophi had vociferously protested her innocence. Ruth Ellis merely said: 'I am guilty.'

She went on: 'I am rather confused.' (At the trial Davies was to say that she showed no sign of confusion, and was very composed.) Thereafter, at Crawford's invitation, she made as voluntary a confession as any murderer has ever made.

There were, however, a few deliberate gaps. She omitted Desmond Cussen's name altogether; she said that she had taken a taxi to Hampstead on Good Friday evening, but did not mention her activities on the Saturday. Most of Easter Sunday also was blank: 'I waited all day today for David to phone but he did not do so. About eight o'clock this evening I put my son Andria to bed. I then took a gun which I had hidden and put it in my handbag.'

In 1955 the Judges' Rules did not permit officers to ask prisoners questions about their statements except for the purpose of removing ambiguity in what had already been said. But the Rules are discretionary guides, not mandatory laws, and this rule was often stretched a good deal if the prisoner did not have a solicitor present. The questions put to Ruth, while not given, are easily reconstructed from her statement. *Where had she obtained the gun?* 'It was given to me by a man in a club.' *Who was the man?* 'I don't remember his name.' *How long ago?* 'About three years.' *Why had he given it to her?* 'It was security for money, but I accepted it as a curiosity.' *Had she known that it was loaded?* 'Not when it was given to me.' *When had she found out?* 'Next morning when I looked at it.'

And the final question: *When you put the gun in your handbag this evening, what did you intend to do?*

'I intended to find David and shoot him.'

Thus willingly Ruth Ellis tightened the noose round her neck. Clearly, when she had killed Blakely she had meant to end it all for both of them.

None of the detectives believed her account of how she had come by the gun. Quite apart from the fact that the story itself was unlikely, the weapon was too clean and well-oiled to have been left without attention for three years. The officers assumed that she wanted to shield the person from whom she had bought, borrowed or stolen the gun, and who might be liable to a charge of unlawful possession. It was a far from uncommon, .38 calibre, 6-shot Smith & Wesson, and its history would be hard to trace.

They examined it in turn, as carelessly unthinking about fingerprints as Alan Thompson had been, for this looked to be an open-and-shut murder case. There was no mystery to solve, no criminal to hunt—just a lot of hard work ahead to gather all the evidence that might be needed for a conviction.

Two officers were taking statements from the Findlaters before midnight, and Ruth's attempt to save Desmond Cussen from embarrassment had failed; the police telephoned his flat to tell him the news. Other officers went to see Ruth's parents, who were unexpectedly close at hand because, for the last few months, they had been living in Ferncroft Avenue, Hampstead, a bare mile from the Magdala. In the morning, Cussen collected the parents and Andria, then drove them to London Bridge Station to take a train to the Midlands. The Neilsons left Andria with a sister of Ruth's and themselves went to Hemel Hempstead to stay with their son Granville.

A post-mortem examination of Blakely's body at 9.30 am showed that one—or perhaps two—of the six bullets fired had grazed the skin, while two had caused the fatal injuries. Death was due to shock and haemorrhage.

The examination was watched by Detective Chief Inspector Leslie Davies and Detective Constable George Claiden, the officers who were to be in charge of the case. Claiden took possession of a spent bullet from the body, a sample of blood, two samples of stomach contents, some tablets from Blakely's pocket, and four garments with bullet holes. Later, he took all these articles, with the gun, to the Metropolitan Police Laboratory at Scotland Yard.

Davies went back to Hampstead Police Station and saw Ruth at 12.30 pm. 'As a result of a post-mortem examination conducted on the body of David Blakely,' he said, 'you will be charged with murdering him.' He then once more cautioned her, charged her, and cautioned her again. To all of this she said just one word: 'Thanks.'

Cussen called at the station to make a statement concerning his relationship with Ruth. He told the police that she had not taken a taxi on Good Friday evening, as she had said, but that he had driven her to Hampstead and waited while she pushed in Blakely's car windows. He also said that Ruth and Andria had spent part of Easter Sunday in his flat, where she had cooked a meal.

> I drove them back to her room about 7.30 pm and that is the last I saw of her . . . During the day there was some slight reference to David, but Ruth certainly did not mention any intention of harming him . . . Although she has lived with me, at no time have I seen a gun in Ruth's possession, nor have I heard her talk about one.

CID officers took statements from the eye-witnesses. Mrs Gladys Yule said that a bullet had passed through the base of her thumb when she was about twenty yards from the Magdala. Her husband had hailed a passing taxi, but the driver had not been keen on taking a fare dripping blood; Mrs Yule had insisted, but co-operatively rode with her hand out of the window. At Hampstead General Hospital they had found a fracture of the first metacarpal bone and prognosed a permanent stiffness of the thumb.

In the afternoon, Findlater was taken to Hampstead Mortuary, New End, where he identified the body. Ruth appeared at Hampstead Magistrates' Court, specially convened because it was a bank holiday, and there Davies gave evidence of her arrest. She was remanded in custody to appear at the same court on 20 April, and then was taken to Holloway Prison, where she asked for a photograph of David Blakely and a copy of the Bible.

There was a newspaper strike in London, so Leon Simmons, senior legal executive for Ruth's solicitor, Victor Mishcon, had no idea why his client failed to keep her Tuesday appointment until another solicitor telephoned. This was John Bickford, of Cardew-Smith & Ross, who had been asked to act for Ruth. He was telephoning as a matter of professional etiquette. Since Victor Mishcon's firm did not handle criminal work, Simmons had no objection to Bickford's acting in her defence.

At about this time, Ruth was writing a letter to Blakely's mother that suggested that she did not want any defenders.

13/4/55

In replying to this letter, please write on the envelope:—

Number 9656 Name R. Ellis

H.M. PRISON HOLLOWAY, N.7. Prison

12. 4. 55

Dear Mrs Cook,

No dought these last few days have been a shock to you
Please try to belive me, when I say, how deeply sorry I am to have caused you this unpleasantness.
No dought you will hear all kinds of stories, regarding David and I
Please do forgive him for decieving you, has regarding myself.
David and I have spent many happy time's together.
Thursday 7th April, David arrived home at 7.15, p.m, he gave me the latest photograph he had, a few days hence had taken, he told me he had given you one.
Friday morning at 10'clock he left and promised to return at 8'clock, but never did
The two people I blame for David's

No. 243 (21442—3-11-42)

death, and my own, are the Finlaytens
No dought you will not undestand this
but perhaps before I hang you will
know what I mean.
Please excuse my writing, but the pen
is shocking.
I implored you to try to forgive David
for living with me, but we were
very much in love with one and other
unfortunately David was not satisfied
with one, woman in his life.
I have forgiven David, I only wish I
could have found it in my heart, to
have forgiven when he was alive.
Once again, I say I am very
sorry to have caused you this misery
and heartache.
I shall die loving your son, And
you should feel content that his death
has been repaid.
Goodbye.
Ruth Ellis

Dear Mrs Cook,
No dought these last few days have been a shock to you
Please try to believe me, when I say, how deeply sorry I am to have caused you this unpleasantness.
No dought you will hear all kinds of stories, regarding David and I. Please do forgive him for decieving you, has regarding myself.
David and I have spent many happy times together.
Thursday 7th April, David arrived home at 7.15., p.m., he gave me the latest photograph he had, a few days hence had taken, he told me he had given you one.
Friday morning at 10 o'clock he left and promised to return at 8 o'clock, but never did. The two people I blame for David's death, and my own, are the Finlayters. No dought you will not understand this but perhaps before I hang you will know what I mean.
Please excuse my writing, but the pen is shocking.
I implore you to try to forgive David for living with me, but we were very much in love with one and other unfortunately David was not satisfied with one woman in his life.
I have forgiven David, I only wish I could have found it in my heart to have forgiven when he was alive.
Once again, I say I am very sorry to have caused you this misery and heartache.
I shall die loving your son. And you should feel content that his death has been repaid.
Goodbye. RUTH ELLIS

In fact, Ruth was over-confident in taking it for granted that she would be executed. Her crime might appear to be a clear case of murder, and certainly in 1955 death was the only statutory punishment for that; but most murderers were not hanged, and statistically her chances of survival were excellent.

In England and Wales there was an annual average of about 150 murders known to the police. Of the 100 or so murderers who did not commit suicide, only about twelve were hanged; and the quota of females was much smaller than that of males.

Of those who were not hanged, a few either escaped arrest entirely or were tried but acquitted because of insufficient evidence. Many more were beneficiaries of perverse jury verdicts, the proportion of acquittals to convictions in some years being as high as one to four, a higher ratio than for almost any other crime. It seems evident that juries managed to find reasonable doubt where it did not exist in cases where they considered the death penalty too severe, and in many other such cases returned verdicts of 'guilty but insane' or 'guilty of manslaughter' that could not possibly be justified in law. Of those who were unqualifiedly convicted of murder and sentenced to death, an additional few were reprieved on the advice of the Home Secretary, who did not have to justify his decision. Thus mercy was shown, in one way or another, to all but a handful of people who had committed the capital crime of murder.

From the foregoing it will be seen that John Bickford, before his first meeting with Ruth Ellis, must have believed that there was a good chance of saving her life. He was assuming, of course, that she *wanted* to live.

As we shall see, he had to wait a week before he was allowed to read her statement to the police. But she recalled for him the gist of at least one sentence from it: 'When I put the gun in my bag, I intended to find David and shoot him.' And, she told Bickford, she would say the same at the trial if she were asked—as he knew she would be, even though the Crown put no other questions.

He was sure, too, that the judge would focus on her intention as the crucial issue. Since she had made six closely successive attempts to carry out an intention to kill, not even the most kindly disposed jury could find the barest possibility that the gun had gone off by accident, or that she had only tried to frighten Blakely by shooting over his head. Insanity was the obvious plea.

The legal definition of insanity was enshrined in the M'Naghten Rules, which had been drawn up by fourteen judges without medical advice in 1843. Under this precise, narrow definition, Ruth Ellis was clearly not insane. In the unchallenged opinion of one Victorian judge, Lord Bramwell, almost nobody was: 'The present law lays down such a definition of madness that nobody is hardly ever really mad enough to be within it—yet it is a logical and good definition.' Many juries, while accepting the first part of Lord Bramwell's opinion, could not agree with the second. In the decade 1940–49 more than 50 per cent of those not acquitted of murder were found by juries to be either 'insane on arraignment' (unfit to plead) or 'guilty but insane',* although hardly any

* The inherently illogical verdict of 'guilty but insane' was changed by the Criminal Procedure (Insanity) Act 1964, section 1, to 'not guilty by reason of insanity'.

of them came under the definitions in the M'Naghten Rules. And of those whose plea of insanity was rejected by the jury, some were reprieved as mentally unfit on the advice of the Home Secretary, who was not even theoretically bound by the Rules.

But when Bickford explained to Ruth that her best chance lay in a plea of insanity, she flatly refused to countenance the idea. Later, when her mother tried to persuade her to accept her solicitor's advice, she said: 'It's no good. I was sane when I did it, and I meant to do it.'

In consequence, the only defence seemingly open was manslaughter. On the face of it, again, this looked hopeless, because English law did not yet, as Scotland's did, recognise the defence of diminished responsibility. Still, as the Lord Chief Justice, Lord Goddard, had told the Royal Commission on Capital Punishment of 1949–53 (Cmd. 8932), 'You get verdicts of manslaughter in quite astonishing cases.' One such case, which occurred in 1951, is recorded in Anthony Babington's *The Power to Silence* (Maxwell, 1967). A young woman was charged with the murder of her baby, and her counsel belatedly suggested that if the jury could not acquit her, they should convict her only of manslaughter. Though the judge predictably told the jury that 'there was no evidence before them on which they could possibly reach such a verdict', they accepted defence counsel's suggestion, and the woman was sentenced merely to a short term of imprisonment.

Even should Ruth Ellis's jury pay more heed to the judge, who would probably tell them that a verdict of manslaughter was unwarranted, the evidence might still induce them to recommend mercy. This would perhaps increase her chances of a reprieve, although it would not guarantee it. Statistically, an average of seven and a half murderers were recommended for mercy each year, and of these two and a half were nevertheless hanged; Mrs Styllou Christophi was one of the unlucky third in 1954.

But Ruth Ellis did not want mercy. She was no more willing to ask for pity than to give it. 'An eye for an eye, a life for a life,' she told Bickford. 'I took David's life, and I don't ask you to save mine. I don't want to live.'

'Is it not possible,' suggested a correspondent in *The Lancet* after the execution (*see Appendix 3*), 'that Ruth Ellis had suicidal urges and wanted to die?'

It was not merely possible, or even probable, but virtually certain. It was also unremarkable, since Ruth's suicidal urges, far from being exceptional, were (and are) shared by most English murderers.

No fewer than one-third of them actually killed themselves;* others tried but were prevented, or bungled it; still others meant to do it but lost their nerve. Some, perhaps most, of the failed suicides were either found guilty but insane or were reprieved. Even so, more than one out of five of all persons hanged had either attempted suicide, pleaded guilty despite the judge's warning of the inevitable consequences, or asked to be hanged: such suicidal urges were manifested by twenty-two of the last 100 murderers to be hanged before the death penalty was restricted by the Homicide Act of 1957. To at least one of these, who was sentenced to death just two weeks after Ruth Ellis, execution was the sole incentive to the crime. Frederick Cross of Uttoxeter told the police that he had no other motive for the murder of a complete stranger: 'I killed him so I would be hanged.' At his trial he insisted on pleading guilty, and afterwards refused to appeal or to ask for a reprieve. As *The Lancet* correspondent observed: 'his desire to die was granted by a benevolent state'.

Suicide was certainly not Ruth's only motive, but it was part of her aim. She shot Blakely to end his life and hers. If the death penalty had already been abolished, she would perhaps still have done it, but saved a bullet or two for herself. If anything might have deterred her it was the fear of a long term of imprisonment; as she told her mother during Mrs Neilson's first visit: 'I won't go to prison for ten years or more and come out old and finished. I'd rather be hanged.'

It is, of course, always difficult to build up a case for a client who wants the maximum punishment. Why should Ruth Ellis bother to say anything to her solicitor or give evidence at her trial? She might as well plead guilty and get it over quickly, like

* This is a curious constant that has not been affected by changes in the punishment for the crime. In the twelve years 1957–68 there were 1,570 cases of murder in England and Wales known to the police, and in 566 of these the suspects committed suicide. The figures are from *Murder 1957 to 1968* (HMSO, 1969).

Frederick Cross. But Bickford found her quite willing to talk, for a reason of her own: she wanted to prove that she had been morally justified in killing David Blakely—that, as she had perhaps sung when a crooner with a dance band,

He was her man
And he done her wrong.

This was what she wanted her lawyers to prove at the trial.

The gap at the end of her story, from Good Friday to the evening of Easter Sunday, disturbed Bickford more than it did the police. It would be difficult to argue a spur-of-the-moment killing, an uncontrollable impulse due to extreme provocation, if she had delayed nearly forty-eight hours after the last time she had been provoked. The fact that, equally, it would not add to her moral justification if she kept silent persuaded her to tell Bickford what had happened after lunch on the Saturday.

Andria had gone to the zoo alone, and at about two o'clock Cussen had driven Ruth to Hampstead, where they saw Blakely's Vanguard parked outside the Magdala. Ruth told Cussen to drive on to Tanza Road. Across the road from the Findlaters' she saw workmen going in and out of a ground-floor flat; she learnt that it was for sale. Soon she was having a cup of tea with the owner, sitting by the front window. She saw the Findlaters and Blakely come back from the Magdala soon after closing time. An hour later, at about four, they reappeared in the street, this time with a girl holding a baby, and drove off in a car. It was Ruth's first glimpse of the new nanny. On the way home she told Cussen that she was sure that David was having an affair with the girl.

After supper, she put Andria to bed and asked Cussen to drive her back to Tanza Road. Blakely's car was outside the Findlaters'. Ruth stood at the side of the house and saw more cars drive up. She heard Blakely's laugh and a woman's giggle, then Blakely came out with a young, dark woman whom Ruth thought was the nanny but could not be sure. She heard Blakely say: 'Let me put my arm round you for support.' He showed the girl the car windows that Ruth had pushed in, then he and the girl and Findlater drove off in another car. Ruth went away, but returned and saw that the car was back. Again she heard Blakely laugh and a woman giggle. At about 12.30 am on Sunday morning a window blind was pulled down and the light went out in the hall. Seething with jealousy, Ruth drove back to Egerton Gardens in Cussen's car.

About Easter Sunday, Ruth had nothing more to say. She had telephoned Findlater just before nine o'clock in the morning. After that, she had done nothing of importance until, at around 8 pm, she had taken a taxi to Hampstead and killed Blakely.

This did not seem at all plausible. The fact that she had nothing to gain for herself by concealing the whole truth indicated that she was protecting someone else.

Then there was the source of the gun. She stuck to the highly unlikely story that she had told the police. Again the inference was likely that she was shielding someone. The same person, then? If so, it seemed probable that she was not merely shielding him from a charge of unlawful possession.

So, from the very start of the case, there was a presumption that Ruth Ellis might be protecting someone who had helped her to commit the crime: an abettor, or accessory before the fact, who would be liable to the same charge of murder.

The newspaper strike ended, and many more people learnt of the shooting in Hampstead. Ruth's friends were not surprised that she had wanted to kill David Blakely, only that she had had a gun to do it with. As her old receptionist-artist, Alexander Engleman, said to a former Little Club hostess, Jackie Lockhart, in a chance meeting at a tea-dance at Skindle's, near Maidenhead: 'She wasn't the type of girl to carry a gun about.' When Jacqueline Dyer visited Ruth in prison, she asked about the gun, and heard the same story as had everyone else. But Mrs Dyer knew that it was untrue, since she had helped Ruth with her packing when she left the Little Club and would have seen the gun.

On the other hand, Mrs Marie-Thérèse Harris, of the French Institute, thought that perhaps she *had* seen the gun.

After learning from an evening paper of her former pupil's arrest, Mrs Harris decided that it was her duty to tell someone what she knew. By chance, one of her neighbours was Commander Jones of Special Branch, and she telephoned him at Scotland Yard. The same evening, Detective Constable Claiden called at Mrs Harris's flat just before supper; she remembers him as a pleasant young man who went on talking until she and her husband were faint with hunger, and then Mrs Harris cooked eggs and bacon which all three ate together. Claiden went away with a signed statement by Mrs Harris relating to an occasion when she had given Ruth her lesson in some other man's flat. Mrs Harris said that she had been let in by Andria:

> I asked him for Mrs Ellis's copy book, which I marked for her next lesson, and dated the book. I chatted with the little boy and mentioned that we were troubled by pigeons. He said 'What you want is a gun', and with that he opened the drawer of the table on which I was writing. In the drawer I noticed, among other things, two guns, which at first I thought were his toys. He handled one, the larger one, then said 'It's all right, it's not loaded'. Then he put it back and closed the drawer and I left.

On Monday, 18 April, Davies and Claiden went to see the other man, whom we shall call X, in his flat. Davies asked him if he had ever given a revolver to Ruth Ellis. He said that he had not. Had he ever had a revolver? No. Then Davies told him that two guns had recently been seen in a drawer at his flat.

X opened the table drawer, which contained one gun, a Webley air pistol. He said that he could not explain how two guns could have been seen. Then he searched all his drawers, and at last found an 'Em-ge' starter's pistol which fired blank caps.

Davies and Claiden did not take a written statement from X, but they went away with the two pistols. Then they called on Mrs Harris and asked her to try to identify the guns she had seen briefly three months before. She and her husband both recollect that the detectives showed her three or four guns and asked her to pick the two out.* The guns shown to her evidently did not include the murder weapon, as this was in the Metropolitan Police Laboratory at the time.

After leaving Mrs Harris, who was not asked for a further written statement, Davies sent Claiden to the police laboratory with the Webley air pistol and a request to compare the oil on it with that in the murder gun. The examination was carried out the following day, but the results were inconclusive; in his report, Dr Lewis Nickolls, the director of the laboratory, stated that the

*Editors' note: at a recent meeting, Mrs Harris told us that she knew far too little about firearms to be able to distinguish between one gun and another, and so was unable to assist the detectives.

oil on the Smith & Wesson revolver used in the shooting 'is similar to the oil on the Webley air pistol, but it is not possible to say whether they are the same oils'.

At about this time, Davies conferred with the clerk to the Hampstead magistrates regarding the date for the committal proceedings. They agreed on Thursday, 28 April, when a special court would be convened and the whole day set aside for the hearing. Ruth Ellis reappeared in court on 20 April, but only to be remanded in custody again. John Bickford, who represented her for the first time, applied for copies of statements made by Ruth and by any other witnesses 'who can speak to the background of the lives of these two persons', and Davies told the court that he would bring the request to the notice of the Director of Public Prosecutions.

After the hearing, Davies completed his report on the case, which was submitted, with twenty-six witness statements, to the Assistant Commissioner, 'C' Department (the CID), and thence to the DPP.

Davies's opinion of the case came at the end of the report:

> This is clearly a case of jealousy on the part of Ellis, coupled with the fear that Blakely was leaving her. In spite of what Cussen says, that Ellis wanted to be rid of Blakely and he would not leave, the weight of evidence points quite clearly to the position being completely reversed. The two people, Blakely and Ellis, are of completely different stations in life.

Ruth Ellis's mother, Davies said, was earning thirty shillings a week as a cook and general domestic servant, and her father £4 5s 0d a week as an animal attendant at a laboratory. After referring to Ruth's humble beginnings, Davies went on:

> This girl is considered by her parents to have done very well for herself. However, they both agree that their daughter has always had a violent temper. On meeting Blakely and realising that his class was much above her own, and finding he was sufficiently interested in her to live with her and, if we are to believe Cussen, to promise her marriage, it seems she was prepared to go to any lengths to keep him. Finding this impossible, she appears to have decided to wreak her vengeance upon him.

The inspector went on to say that he believed that Blakely had returned to live with Ellis 'in order to prevent her creating any further disturbances as far as his friends were concerned'.

> However, it seems that in spite of going back with her, Blakely did not intend that this arrangement should last very long, and it was when she decided that he had left her following Good Friday that she made up her mind to take this drastic step. It is certain that her action was coldly premeditated because, without thought to her son, to whom she is said to be very attached, she left him alone to come to Hampstead with her mind made up to commit this murder.

Davies included a short paragraph about the source of the gun:

> Efforts have been made to trace from whom Mrs Ellis obtained the revolver used by her in this offence, but so far without success. Inquiries are being continued with this end in view because I find it difficult to believe her story that she received it as a security for money she had loaned to a man and because it was a curiosity.

Mrs Harris's statement was not included with the report, and Davies did not mention her evidence; but evidently a copy of the statement was passed to Ruth's solicitors, for Mrs Harris recalls having been interviewed by them and subpoenaed for the defence (though, as it turned out, she was not called).

It has been said that an English trial is a contest, not an inquisition; for the sake of fair play, the contestant who is provided with all the resources is expected to help the contestant who has none. Lord Devlin explained this part of the system in a series of lectures to the students of Yale University Law School, which were subsequently published under the title of *The Criminal Prosecution in England* (OUP, 1960):

> It is recognised that to a large but undefined extent the prosecution have the duty of making inquiries for the benefit of both sides. This flows from the principle that the duty of the prosecution is to get at the true facts and bring them before the court and not just to obtain a conviction. This fundamental duty, which is at the root of the whole question, is willingly accepted by the police.

In 1966, Geoffrey Lane, QC, representing the Metropolitan Police at the inquiry into the case of Timothy John Evans (Cmd. 3101), suggested that the duty was smaller but clearly defined:

> It is no part of the function of the police to furnish information to the solicitor for the defence. If any salient matters and relevant facts come to light, the police must inform the Director of Public Prosecutions, and he can then decide what steps should be taken to furnish the defence with the information he has. It is not the duty of the police to provide the names of possible witnesses to the defence, and certainly not to provide witnesses' statements to the defence.

And that, of course, is why Bertrand Russell thought that there should be two police forces, the second one being designed to prove innocence instead of guilt.

A possible weakness in the system is that it does not, and could not reasonably, oblige the police to report salient non-matters and relevant non-facts. Mrs Harris's information about the guns was passed to the defence because there was a statement of evidence to pass; but many police inquiries ended in completely negative results and therefore were not mentioned.

It was nobody's fault that the defence were not told that the driver of Ruth's taxi had never been traced—yet this almost certainly meant that she had been driven in a private car by someone who was keeping quiet, for the Metropolitan Police have an established routine for making inquiries among London cabbies. Indeed, in this case it would have been hardly necessary to inquire: Easter Sunday is not a busy time for London taxis, and no cabby could have failed to remember taking a young platinum-blonde, alone, from Kensington to Hampstead—quite a long journey—about an hour before a man was shot dead in the same part of Hampstead by a young platinum-blonde; he would have talked of little else for weeks.

Ruth Ellis would not have said that she had gone by taxi if she had taken a bus or train, and it was certainly too far to walk. That left only a private car.

She could only have lied about the means of transport in order to shield the driver. She was also shielding the person from whom she had obtained the gun, and probably the person with whom she had spent part of the time between 9 am and 8 pm. Three persons, two, or one?

It was by Ruth's choice that the jury were not told anything of this. Of course, even if they had been told, it would not have altered the fact that she had intentionally killed Blakely. But one wonders, would the verdict have been the same if the jury had known that she had spent part of the day with a man who had a car, that he had given her the gun, and that he had driven her to the scene of the crime that she intended to commit? Or might the jury have found it in their hearts at least to recommend her for mercy?

At the committal proceedings, Ruth Ellis was represented by Mr (now Sir) Sebag Shaw. He entered the formal plea of not guilty, and afterwards saw her in an interview room. He recalls that she was smoking a cigarette in a long holder. She was very angry with him: 'Why do you say I'm not guilty when I am?' she asked. 'I killed him, and I've got to die for it.'

Unknown to Ruth, in another interview room her former husband was saying, or rather shouting, that he wanted to give evidence on her behalf. George Ellis, very drunk, would have burst into the court if he had not been diverted at the door; the defence solicitors calmed him and took a statement from him, but decided that he was not at all likely to help her case. Eventually he was led away by a reporter for the *Sunday Pictorial*, the paper that had bought the story of his life with Ruth. In a sober moment, Ellis stopped publication, not for her sake but for his: he was Chief Dental Officer for Warrington, and he feared that the publicity might ruin him professionally. In fact, ruin was not far off. He lost his job, and three years later was convicted of drunkenness and a breach of the peace; two years after that, he strangled himself in a Jersey hotel when unable to pay the bill. The *Sunday Pictorial* published extracts from his story after his death; his recriminations, which he had originally consented to having published before the decision on reprieve, at least showed that he had not married beneath him. Only one person in this chronicle was lower than George Ellis.

Ruth also was persuaded to sell her life story to another newspaper in the same group. It seems that she misunderstood the terms: the only reason she had for wanting money was to leave it to her son, but apparently she was a party to the more usual deal under which the newspaper paid for the defence.

On 11 May, Ruth Ellis was arraigned at the Central Criminal Court before Mr Justice Barrie. The Crown was represented by Mr Christmas Humphreys, the son of Sir Travers Humphreys, who had been Senior Prosecuting Counsel at the Old Bailey for five years. Leading counsel for the defence was Mr (now Sir) Melford Stevenson. He applied for the case to be put over to the next session, which was to begin on 14 June, on the grounds that many inquiries had still to be made by the defence. Granville Neilson recalls that this was a polite but necessary fiction, and says that the true reason was that the defence hoped for a more broad-minded judge. Edith Thompson, hanged in 1923 for helping her lover murder her husband, had perhaps lost her life because Mr Justice Shearman considered the Seventh Commandment as important as the Sixth. But no similar views had ever been attributed to Mr Justice Barrie, a reputedly kind and sympathetic man. Granville Neilson may have been misinformed. It was only two weeks since the committal proceedings, and at least one of the defence lawyers' inquiries was certainly still unfinished. This was the search for a precedent.

Melford Stevenson was going to ask for the charge to be reduced to manslaughter on the grounds that the accused had been so provoked by jealousy that she had lost her self-control. It was often said that English law did not allow the defence of *crime passionel*, but that was not strictly true. Provocation had been pleaded successfully in cases where a man had discovered his wife in the act of adultery and killed her on the spot, a *crime passionel* if ever there was one; the same defence had been admitted when the adultery had been discovered immediately after rather than during the act. It had been ruled that a wife could be equally provoked by her husband's adultery. In some cases the defence had been successfully extended to couples who were not married but were living together.

Might not a woman be equally provoked by pure jealousy? Had the question ever been considered by a court? Ruth's lawyers were industriously searching the records, not only in England but also in the United States, and this may have been why Melford Stevenson asked for the trial to be postponed.

Mr Justice Barrie granted the application, thereby adding forty days to Ruth Ellis's life.

Forty days is a long time for a platinum-blonde, and Ruth's hair was already dark at the roots. The fact that prison regulations did not allow a man from Shack's in Shaftesbury Avenue to come in and dye her hair was one of her two main preoccupations when she was examined on 4 June by Dr Duncan Whittaker, a psychiatrist acting for the defence. Her other concern was the 24-hour race at Le Mans, to which Blakely had promised to take her. Visitors who expected to find her at least apprehensive about her trial were staggered by her animated questions on the fortunes of the racing drivers she knew.

On 9 and 10 June she was examined by another psychiatrist, retained by the Director of Public Prosecutions. She told him, as she had told Dr Whittaker, that she felt no regret for killing Blakely but considered herself completely justified.

She told her lawyers the same when they called to discuss her defence. Melford Stevenson and Sebag Shaw had been joined by a third counsel, Peter Rawlinson, a future Attorney-General who was then libel reader for the *Daily Mirror* newspaper group, which was paying for Ruth's defence. Sir Peter, as he is now, remembers it as 'a very distressing trial—there really did not seem to be any defence to the charge'. This was evidently not Melford Stevenson's opinion at the time. The search for a precedent had failed; it seemed that no court had ever been asked to consider the defence of provocation by jealousy—which, as the trial judge was to say, was 'very curious after all these years, because jealousy is one of the commonest emotions'. Even so, there still seemed to be a good chance that a jury would accept the defence simply in order to save Ruth from being hanged. The question was whether it would be put to her jury.

Originally, the defence of provocation had been a matter of law: the judge, not the jury, decided whether the provocation was sufficient to reduce the homicide to manslaughter. But judges had gradually developed the practice of leaving the decision to the jury, and this had become the established rule although it had not received statutory confirmation in 1955. (It was confirmed two years later [Homicide Act 1957, section 3].) However, the judge would still have to decide if there was enough evidence of provocation for the matter to be left to the jury. This was the hurdle that Melford Stevenson had to try to clear.

These legal niceties did not interest Ruth. 'All I want is that the jury should hear my full story,' she wrote to a friend shortly before the trial. She no longer cared about fixing blame on the Findlaters; no one else mattered—even Cussen did not count. There were only two persons involved, and soon both would be dead; she just wanted to prove first that David Blakely had 'asked for it' and that she had had the right to kill him. It was not a point of view likely to soften the hearts of the jury. Nor was her manner or appearance. Instead of looking dejected, meek and pathetic, she was cool, proud and self-possessed.

The Governor of Holloway, Dr Charity Taylor, had been christened more appropriately than her prisoner. A few days before the trial, she allowed Shack's to send in materials and instructions for one of the wardresses to dye and set Ruth's hair. The platinum result delighted Ruth but probably dismayed her lawyers. An aspirant for mercy could do her cause no good by looking radiant.

The trial began in No. 1 Court at the Old Bailey on Monday, 20 June 1955, before Mr Justice Havers. Christmas Humphreys, prosecuting, was assisted by Mervyn Griffith-Jones and Miss Jean Southworth.

Ruth Ellis came up from the cells like a film-star. She wore a black suit with astrakhan-fur trimmings, and her hair was impeccably blonde. She smiled reassuringly at the small woman in blue beside her, her favourite wardress at Holloway who had been sent to the trial at Ruth's request.

Mr Humphreys began his opening speech by introducing the accused as a divorced woman who in 1954 and 1955 was having simultaneous love affairs with two men. 'It would seem that, lately, Blakely, the deceased man, was trying to break off the connection, and that the accused woman was angry at the thought that he should leave her, even though she had another lover at the time.' This misleading version of the story was to be corrected by the evidence, and by the judge in his summing-up, but first impressions persist because the mind tends to absorb them preferentially; that is doubtless why opening speeches are not a part of Scottish criminal trials. After giving more—and more misleading—details about Ruth's love life, Mr Humphreys told the jury not to let any of this prejudice them against her: '. . . you are not here in the least concerned with adultery or any sexual misconduct. You are not trying for immorality but for murder, and the only importance of these movements between her and these various men is that it will help you to see the frame of mind she was in when she did what it cannot be denied in fact she did.'

None of the prosecution witnesses was in the witness box for long; few were detained by cross-examination. As Mr Stevenson later made clear, he deliberately abstained from attempting to probe the accuracy, or the motives, of the principal witnesses.

As the evidence was given, Ruth Ellis sat quite still in the dock. Sir Peter Rawlinson recalls having been 'impressed by her detachment from all that was going on'.

The case for the Crown was completed before the luncheon adjournment, and Melford Stevenson rose to make his opening speech for the defence. He said that Ruth had been driven to kill Blakely by the sufferings he had inflicted on her; when she committed the crime, her judgment was unseated and her understanding gone, so that malice was absent. He called the defendant to give evidence on her own behalf.

Ruth and her counsel were probably equally disappointed in each other's showing in evidence-in-chief. She thought he asked the wrong questions. He must have been dismayed by her casual, offhand answers. The Americans have a saying, 'walking on wall-to-wall eggs', and this seems an adequate description of Mr Stevenson's problem; he never knew quite what to expect. At one point, he asked Ruth what she had done on Easter Sunday evening after Cussen had brought her home.

'I put my son to bed.'

'Yes. Go on.'

'I was very upset, and I had a peculiar idea I wanted to kill him [Blakely].'

'You had what?'

'I had an idea I wanted to kill him.' It was a reply that was to be quoted against her in the judge's summing-up.

No doubt Ruth made a poor impression on the jury, appearing callous and immoral. Yet in the whole of her evidence there is not a mean or vindictive word against anyone. She did not mention the Findlaters; she said nothing spiteful about their new nanny; she co-operated when her counsel asked her not to name the married woman Blakely had slept with at Penn. And she could not quite bring herself to castigate Blakely. She almost apologised for all the bruises Cussen had spoken about: 'He only used to hit me with his fists and hands, but I bruise very easily, and I was full of bruises on many occasions.' She would not definitely blame him for her last miscarriage: 'Well, we had a fight a few days previously—I forget the exact time—and David got very, very violent. I do not know whether that caused the miscarriage or not, but he did thump me in the tummy.'

Christmas Humphreys asked her only one question, the inevitable one:

'Mrs Ellis, when you fired that revolver at close range into the body of David Blakely, what did you intend to do?'

'It is obvious that when I shot him I intended to kill him.'

'Thank you,' said Mr Humphreys, and sat down.

The only other witness for the defence was Dr Duncan Whittaker, who gave his opinion that women were more prone to hysterical reactions than men, and more dangerous when hysterical: 'They are inclined to lose some of their inhibitory capacity and solve their problems on a more primitive level.'

When Dr Whittaker had left the witness box, Mr Justice Havers dismissed the jury, and Melford Stevenson argued his case for putting to them the defence of provocation by jealousy. 'But that is new law!' exclaimed the judge. Mr Stevenson persisted, Mr Humphreys argued against him, and the judge promised to give his ruling the next morning.

The ruling went against the defence. Mr Stevenson then said that it would be improper for him to address the jury again. Mr Humphreys also waived his right to a final speech.

In summing-up, Mr Justice Havers began by telling the jury not to let themselves be influenced by sympathy for the accused or the consequences of their verdict. He said that the crucial issue was Ruth's intention, and advised the jury: 'It is not open to you to bring in a verdict of manslaughter on the grounds of provocation.' Even if they accepted every word of Ruth's evidence, he said, it did not establish any sort of defence to the charge of murder. 'If you are satisfied that the accused deliberately fired those shots at Blakely, and as a result he died, it is not open to you to find a verdict of not guilty.'

The jury were out for twenty-three minutes. Their verdict was Guilty with no recommendation for mercy. When the Clerk asked Ruth Ellis if she had anything to say, she did not answer. The black cap was put on the judge's wig, and he sentenced her to death. As he said: '. . . and may the Lord have mercy on your soul', she bowed her head as if in church and then turned smartly from the dock. One of the two wardresses reached out a hand to help but she gently brushed it aside. With a brief encouraging smile to her relatives and friends at the back of the court, she walked down the steps to the cells. It was all over before lunch on the second day.

Neither side had mentioned the missing pieces of evidence: not a word about Ruth's activities on Easter Sunday, or the missing cabby, or the truth about the gun. Ruth had simply repeated her original story about the gun, and no more questions had been asked. After the trial, Inspector Davies asked Mrs Dyer if she had any idea where the gun had come from, and she said she had not. A journalist writing in the *Evening News* took Ruth's evidence at face value: 'The man who gave it to her has never been named, but it is believed he was an army officer . . . Possibly Mrs Ellis may have forgotten the identity of the man who made that illegal transaction.' *The public at large had not the slightest suspicion that Ruth Ellis might have had an accomplice.*

She was taken back to Holloway, and put first in the hospital wing, where her parents and her brother Granville visited her. She told them, as she had already told her lawyers, that she did not intend to appeal. As they were leaving, she thrust a scrap of paper into Granville Neilson's hand. He looked at it outside the prison and saw it was a request for a lethal drug. He showed it to his father, who thought they ought to try to get the drug for Ruth, but Granville refused and tore up the slip. His task for the next three weeks was to try to get his sister reprieved.

Many foreign commentators were shocked by the sentence. On the day after the trial, Jean Wetz wrote in *Le Monde*:

> English law does not at the moment recognise any intermediate stage between the rational and balanced being who kills in perfect

> awareness of what he is doing and the total lunatic who is not conscious of his own acts. As everyone knows, the Englishman is—or believes himself to be—a creature of *sang-froid*, and the legal system in force supports this fiction in over-ruling once and for all any emotional troubles or irresistible impulses. As seen by the upholders of tradition, the place accorded to so degrading a concept as the *crime passionel* seems precisely to be the true measure of 'French decadence'. But the doubts which begin increasingly to be felt will certainly be stimulated by yesterday's trial.

The difference between the English and French positions was underlined the very next day, when a woman in Corsica was also tried and convicted for the premeditated murder of a lover. She was sentenced to two years' imprisonment with suspension of sentence, and immediately released on probation.

Against Ruth Ellis's wishes, her solicitor, John Bickford, wrote a seven-page letter to the Home Secretary saying why he thought she should be reprieved; and at Bickford's request, Leon Simmons, Victor Mishcon's senior legal executive, also wrote to the Home Secretary, giving details of the unhappiness she had suffered through her marriage.

At the same time, a petition was drawn up and signatures were collected. Bickford was confident ('I couldn't believe they would hang her,' he afterwards said); and, indeed, her chances seemed good. Even Christmas Humphreys, at the trial, had hinted that he thought there were grounds for reprieve: 'I accept that there is full evidence that this woman was disgracefully treated. I accept that it would tend to lead her into an intensely emotional condition. These conditions may apply elsewhere.'

On all this optimism the *Daily Mirror* columnist 'Cassandra' (William Connor) poured cold water: 'Only the Home Secretary can save her . . . it is unlikely that he will do so.' (*See Appendix 1.*)

The Home Secretary was Major Gwilym Lloyd George. Like his famous father, he had once been a Liberal, and after moving to the right he had kept some liberal ideas. In 1948 he had voted in the Commons for the total suspension of the death penalty—but he had not then been Home Secretary, an office with a marked tendency to change its holders' opinions on the matter. Sir Samuel Hoare opposed the death penalty before he became

Home Secretary, supported it when in office, and afterwards (as Lord Templewood) wrote a book against it. Chuter Ede, too, fought for abolition before he took charge of the Home Office, was so obdurate a defender of the death penalty when in office that he declined to advise a reprieve for Timothy Evans, and, when out of office again, returned to the abolitionist ranks. Gwilym Lloyd George himself, in less than a year as Home Secretary, had already shown his change of mettle by declining to advise a reprieve for Mrs Styllou Christophi in spite of a recommendation for mercy from the jury and the prison doctor's opinion that she was insane.

Since Home Secretaries are considered immune to outside influences, the newspapers were free to publish opinions about what he ought to do. The article by 'Cassandra' was entitled 'Should Ruth Ellis Hang?' His own answer was that she should not. Among others, three Members of Parliament, Sir Beverley Baxter, Anthony Greenwood and Emanuel Shinwell, expressed the same opinion in letters to the *Evening Standard* (*see Appendix 2*).

But by no means all the published letters advocated a reprieve. 'The English are much too apt to forget the first corpse,' said Miss Fryn Tennyson Jesse, and pointed out that it was neither here nor there that David Blakely was 'a lamentable specimen of humanity'. This description of Blakely provoked a letter of protest from his brother Derek, who wrote that the many people 'who knew and loved David for years . . . should require a great deal more proof than that provided by the defence at the trial that any of the allegations against his character were founded on fact'.

When Ruth read these letters she was pleased by Derek Blakely's loyalty but disappointed by his disbelief of her side of the case. She was not at all grateful to 'Cassandra' and her other supporters, either. They thought she had been wrong to kill Blakely but that she ought not to be hanged, and she disagreed on both points.

She spent her time in the condemned cell making dolls, doing jigsaw puzzles, reading the Bible, and comforting her visitors. She even jollied Bickford along with a macabre joke: 'I gave

David a lot of rope—come to think of it, he's giving me quite a bit now.'

At her request, and with Bickford's consent, Leon Simmons called to help her draw up her will. It seems likely that she used the will as an excuse for a visit by Simmons, whom she admired and trusted probably more than any other man she ever knew.

Jacqueline Dyer visited her several times and always asked about the gun, for she had never believed Ruth's story. *At last, Ruth said that X had given her the gun and driven her to Hampstead.* Mrs Dyer implored her to give this information to her lawyers, but Ruth not only refused but withdrew her confidence; she went back to her old story about having had the gun hidden, and having taken a taxi to Hampstead.

Mrs Dyer went to her MP. Luckily it was George Rogers. 'I never turn down a request for help if it is in my power to give it,' he said, and this was true. Timothy Evans's mother lived in his constituency, and he had set up the first, private investigation into the Evans-Christie affair.

On 29 June, Rogers went to see Ruth in Holloway. Evidently she made little better impression on him than she had in court. 'Although she was much refined by the weeks of suffering, I thought that in normal conditions she was probably a hard, brassy blonde,' he recalls. 'Of course, as I saw her only once, this opinion is superficial. She certainly had much courage, and had resigned herself to death. She was quite sure she would meet her victim in the next world.' The interview, says Rogers, was 'long and painful'. He was trying to persuade her, as he put it later, to 'make a fight for it', but she was just not interested in fighting. 'I finally persuaded her by arguing that she ought to think of her son and try to live for him.' As Ruth could not find an answer to this, she finally agreed to allow Rogers to ask the Home Secretary for clemency. It took him three-quarters of an hour to extract that concession, and she still refused to repeat what she had told Jacqueline Dyer about the gun.

Rogers wrote to the Home Secretary, saying he had come to the conclusion that there was a case for a reprieve since Mrs Dyer's information threw doubt upon the evidence that the crime was premeditated. He was not granted an interview. Mrs Dyer also wrote to the Home Secretary; she had meanwhile learnt of Mrs

Harris's evidence, and she mentioned that, too. The Home Office sent her letter across Whitehall to Scotland Yard for investigation and report, and from there it was passed to 'S' Division, where it was dealt with by Chief Inspector Davies.

On 1 July, Mrs Dyer made a statement to Davies. She told of her friendship with Ruth and of the time when she had helped her to pack: 'I can honestly say that I saw everything she had. I packed most of the things in her suitcase, and I can swear that there was no gun there.'

She went on:

> David Blakely seemed to me to be a fool of a man who shouldn't go out with a girl like Ruth. He was very jealous of Ruth and was even jealous of me because she thought a lot of me. They quarrelled frequently, and he beat and kicked her. I saw them fighting in the flat one day, and he pushed her out of the flat and she fell down six stairs. She was frequently bruised about the body.
> I had not seen Ruth for about two months before the shooting, but I frequently rang her up, the last occasion being ten days before the affair. On this last occasion she told me that she was very happy and that she and David were going to get married.
> I feel that Ruth shot David because of the way he had treated her and in my opinion he asked for what he got. I wrote to the Home Secretary after I had seen Ruth in prison, because I wanted to help my friend, and because she must have been driven to it by the way Blakely had treated her.
> During one of my visits to Ruth I gathered from her that X had given her the gun, and that he had driven her to Hampstead on the night of the shooting. She later denied that X had given her the gun, but I cannot see who else could have given it to her. I still press the question every time I see Ruth, because I think she is telling lies when she says he did not give it to her. It is also my opinion that Ruth did not go to Hampstead by taxi, but was taken there in X's car.
> I intend to do everything in my power to save my friend's life because I think it is only justice, and I know the life she had to lead with Blakely.

After taking Mrs Dyer's statement, Davies wrote a long and careful report.

> It can be stated here that Ellis's story that she had had the gun in her possession for three years was not believed from the outset because of the clean and well-oiled condition it was in. As a consequence, inquiries were made at that time to trace its origin but without success.

Davies went on to describe his visit with Detective Constable Claiden to X's flat on 18 April:

> After we had made known the reason for our inquiry, X emphatically denied that he had ever given a revolver to Ruth Ellis or in fact that he had ever had one in his possession. When I told him that two guns had been seen in a drawer in his flat he produced a Webley air pistol but was at a loss to explain the two guns that had been seen. However, a search of the drawers revealed that in addition to the air pistol he was also in possession of an 'Em-ge' starter's pistol which fired blank caps. This I took possession of. Later that day I showed these pistols to Mrs Harris and she identified the air pistol and the starter's pistol as being the ones she had seen in the drawer.

Davies did not mention that he had taken the Webley air pistol to the Metropolitan Police Laboratory for comparison of the oil with that in the murder gun.

> During the remand period I several times questioned Ruth Ellis as to the authenticity of her story that the gun was given to her three years ago as a security for money and as a curiosity. Throughout she was adamant that this story was true. In view of this we were forced to accept the fact that X did not give the revolver to her.

Davies summarised Mrs Dyer's statement. Next he turned back to Ruth's statement to the police after her arrest:

> It will be seen that she says that she travelled to Hampstead by taxi cab on the night of the shooting. This taxi cab was never traced, but it is significant that she does not mention her movements on the day of the murder until 8 pm . . . I am of the opinion that X did not supply the gun, neither did he drive Mrs Ellis to Hampstead on that night.

Davies confirmed Mrs Dyer's account of Blakely's physical violence to Ruth, saying that supporting evidence had already been obtained from Dr Hill of Middlesex Hospital. He concluded his report:

> Nothing further calling for inquiry has emerged from the letter of Mrs Dyer, but it is my opinion after seeing her that, being a Frenchwoman, she finds it difficult to believe that Ellis should pay the supreme penalty for a crime of this nature. I think she is genuine in her efforts to save her friend, but unfortunately she cannot say anything that we do not already know and that has not been inquired into.

Davies's opinion was shared by the Home Office, who stated in a minute added to the Ellis file on 1 July:

> It seems . . . that even if Mrs Dyer's theory about the gun is true, it is not directly relevant to the question of premeditation. It does not affect the fact that Mrs Ellis went to Hampstead armed with a gun which she then used against Blakely.

That was the official view. Whether she had taken a gun out of a hiding place and called a taxi, or had had a gun put in her hand and been driven to the scene when she was already hysterical, was not directly relevant to the question of premeditation. The public view might have been different. But the matter was not made public. It was to remain buried, with Jacqueline Dyer's statement, for nearly twenty years.

Five days later, on 6 July, the Home Secretary discovered sufficient grounds to justify advising Her Majesty to interfere with the due course of the law in the case of Mrs Sarah Lloyd, who had murdered a woman of eighty-six by battering her head with a spade. Mrs Lloyd was reprieved exactly one week before the date fixed for Ruth Ellis's execution.

On that day, too, the Home Office received a letter from Alexander Engleman, the former receptionist and artist at the Little Club, one of the many persons who had known Ruth and not thought her the type to carry a gun about. His letter was about the taxi that had never been traced. Private persons sometimes buy retired taxis, and Engleman suggested that Ruth had travelled in one of these. He had little evidence to offer, but his suggestion could not easily be ignored, for the man he named as the possible driver of the taxi was the man Mrs Dyer had named as the owner of the gun.

Engleman's letter was passed to Detective Constable Claiden, who interviewed him on 6 July at his home in Grafton Way, off Tottenham Court Road. Engleman said:

> One evening, I think at the beginning of 1954, when the Little Club was closed, X was there and asked me if he could give me a lift home. I accepted and went downstairs with him. Outside the club I looked for his car, and he pointed to an old taxi which was parked across the road, and said, 'This is my car.' I asked him where his other car was, and he said, 'It's in dock. I've borrowed

> this. Jump in.' He went to the driver's seat and put on a chauffeur's cap, then drove me to his flat, where I went in and had a drink with him. After a while I left him and came home.

Engleman went on to tell of his conversation about the gun, a few days after the shooting, with Jackie Lockhart at Skindle's. As he did not know the girl's surname, Claiden thought at first that he was referring to Jacqueline Dyer, who in fact had never met Engleman as he had left the Little Club before she arrived. The matter was of no importance except that it showed that Engleman knew nothing of Mrs Dyer's intervention about the gun.

After clearing up this confusion, Claiden set off to interrogate X, but he was nowhere to be found; neither that day, nor the next, nor the day after that. As time was running short, Claiden wrote his report on Friday, 8 July, with X still missing and Ruth Ellis having only five more days to live.

> I made inquiries of a number of friends of both Blakely and X, but none could remember X ever having used an old taxi cab. It may well be that he did so when driving Engleman home but it would appear that it was an isolated incident. No information could be obtained concerning the possible ownership of the machine.
>
> X has not been seen, and although intensive inquiries were made to trace him, he could not be found. It is believed that he returned to London during the afternoon of 6 July 1955, but his present whereabouts are unknown. If, within the next few days, X is traced he will be interrogated in respect of the use of the taxi cab with Engleman, and of the possibility that he drove Ellis to the scene of the murder.
>
> Even if it is established that X drove her to Hampstead on that evening, it would have little bearing on the culpability of Ellis in this matter, but so far there is not a shred of evidence to show that X did take her to the scene of the crime.

Engleman's statement and Claiden's report were passed rapidly through the usual channels to the Assistant Commissioner, 'C' Department, and thence to the Home Office, arriving in time to join the rest of the papers in the Ruth Ellis case for the Home Secretary to read over the weekend at the home of his sister, Lady Megan Lloyd George, in Wales.

As the Home Secretary left London, X returned, and Davies

and Claiden went to his flat to ask if he had ever used an old taxi. To their surprise, he said that he had. Claiden took a short statement: '. . . I bought it early in 1954 . . . I ran it for several months until about June 1954, then loaned it to several friends to use on their holidays. Then I disposed of it in about August or September the same year. I have not used it since.' X named the dealer from whom he had bought the taxi, and gave the name and address of the person to whom he had sold it.

Davies and Claiden took the statement on Saturday, 9 July. Thereafter it made slow progress, not reaching the ACC until after Ruth Ellis was dead, and never reaching the Home Office at all. It appears that no one ever tried to verify the date on which X had disposed of the taxi. The Home Secretary still believed that X had never owned a taxi when he came back from Wales on Monday, 11 July, and made the decision whether or not Ruth Ellis should be hanged.

As if to help him make up his mind, the *Evening Standard* published that day a letter from Mrs Gladys Yule:

> Don't let us turn Ruth Ellis into a national heroine. I stood petrified and watched her kill David Blakely in cold blood . . . These hysterical people, getting up petitions for a reprieve, and those rushing to sign them. Do they realise Ruth Ellis shot Blakely to the danger of the public? She might easily have killed me, an innocent passer-by, a complete stranger. As it is I have a partly crippled right hand for life . . . Crime passionel indeed! What if other countries would let her off from her just punishment? When has Britain followed the lead of others? Let us remain a law-abiding country where citizens can live and walk abroad in peace and safety.

If Mrs Yule's letter did not influence the Home Secretary, he was certainly influenced by what had happened to her when he closed the Ruth Ellis file and endorsed it with the traditional formula that he had failed to discover any sufficient ground to justify him in advising Her Majesty to interfere with the due course of the law.

Home Secretaries do not have to justify their decisions about reprieve; but nearly ten years later, Lloyd George (Lord Tenby, as he then was) told Fenton Bresler that he refused a reprieve for Ruth Ellis because of the bullets that had missed:

> We cannot have people shooting off firearms in the street. This was a public thoroughfare where Ruth Ellis stalked [*sic*] and shot her quarry. And remember that she did not only kill David Blakely; she also injured a passer-by. As long as I was Home Secretary I was determined to ensure that people could use the streets without fear of a bullet.

Bresler comments on this:

> By an odd paradox, if Ruth Ellis had been a more accurate shot she probably would not have been hanged. If a stray bullet had not caught Mrs Yule I am almost certain that Lord Tenby would have reprieved her.
> (*Reprieve*, Harrap, 1965.)

At 3.14 pm on Monday, 11 July, a Home Office messenger took a taxi from Whitehall to Holloway, bearing the official refusal of a reprieve.

Shortly afterwards, John Bickford called to see his client, and was given the sack. It was evidently not a matter of cause and effect. About a fortnight earlier, Bickford had told Leon Simmons that he felt that Ruth did not have the same confidence in him as she had in Simmons. If Bickford had done wrong in her eyes, it was in trying too hard. She blamed him, and all her lawyers, for wasting time at the trial by attempting to save her life instead of proving that she had had a right to take Blakely's.

George Rogers called next, with an invitation for Andria to stay with him and his wife for a holiday. 'The boy had been kept in the dark as there was still a little hope,' he recalls, 'and we thought that it would be better to keep him away from his normal surroundings where he might learn the truth rather brutally.' Ruth accepted the invitation, and also told Rogers that she would like to see Leon Simmons again. She did not give a reason.

The request came to Simmons from Bickford, who said that Ruth had lost confidence in him. Simmons discussed the matter with his principal, Victor Mishcon, and they decided that they should both go. They set off next morning, 12 July, still not knowing what she wanted to say—but 'it could be,' said Mishcon, 'that we might be asked to do something'. Therefore, they called first on Bickford, and Mishcon asked him: 'Is there anything in particular we should question her about?'

'Try to find out where and when she got the gun,' Bickford said.

Wearing a dressing gown over her prison clothes, Ruth received them in the condemned cell as if it were her drawing room. 'How kind of you to come,' she said, extending her hand in greeting.

She said that she had certain facts to tell Simmons that might have some bearing on her will, and she clearly thought this was the only matter they had to discuss. But Mishcon asked her if she would not care to tell them about the gun. She refused repeatedly, insisting that she stood by what she had said at the trial.

'I'm not asking for a reprieve,' she said. 'I'm quite composed to the fact that tomorrow is the end. And I believe it is a just end.'

Mishcon was faced with a terrible dilemma. He could see that she was indeed calm and composed. Ought he to risk destroying this composure, which perhaps she needed more than anything, by introducing questions that she appeared to have solved for herself?

It was a considered, positive decision of hers that she wanted to die. Mishcon believed that there were three reasons. The first was the obvious one—that, being young and spirited, the prospect of life imprisonment was more frightening than immediate death. Secondly, she had loved Blakely, and killed him, and without Blakely her reason for living was gone. Finally, she had what Mishcon calls 'a deep, but of course quite individual, moral sense'. She may have been immoral but she was certainly not amoral; she was emotional and loyal and had her own code. 'A life for a life,' she said. 'Isn't that just?'

Looking at her—'young, attractive, a mother'—Mishcon felt that he had to try to save her life. 'Don't you owe it to your son to leave behind you a record of truth?' he asked. 'Shouldn't he hear the true story, in your own words, and not just read about the case in the newspapers?' Simmons, too, tried to make her change her mind.

At last she said: 'You're the only person who has been able to persuade me to do this. I suppose the truth would have been found out anyway after I've gone. I'll tell you what happened if you'll promise not to use it to try and save me.'

'Tell us what happened,' said Mishcon, 'and we can discuss

afterwards whether or not we have your permission to do anything with it.'

'I don't want to get anyone else in trouble—one life for a life is enough,' she said. 'I didn't say anything about it up to now because it seemed traitorous—absolutely traitorous.' Then she began to tell them, and Mishcon wrote it down in statement form:

> I, Ruth Ellis, have been advised by Mr Victor Mishcon to tell the whole truth in regard to the circumstances leading up to the killing of David Blakely and it is only with the greatest reluctance that I have decided to tell how it was that I got the gun with which I shot Blakely. I did not do so before because I felt that I was needlessly getting someone into possible trouble.
>
> I had been drinking Pernod (I think that is how it is spelt) in X's flat and X had been drinking too. This was about 8.30 pm. We had been drinking for some time. I had been telling X about Blakely's treatment of me. I was in a terribly depressed state. All I remember is that X gave me a loaded gun . . . I was in such a dazed state that I cannot remember what was said. I rushed out as soon as he gave me the gun. He stayed in the flat.
>
> I had never seen that gun before. The only gun I had ever seen there was a small air pistol used as a game with a target.

Mishcon read it over to her. (Evidently the French aperitif was not on his personal wine list, so he had asked her to spell the word, which she did correctly but without much confidence, and he included her rider in case she had made a mistake.)

Just before signing the statement, she said: 'There's one more thing. You had better know the whole truth. I rushed back after a second or so and said: "Will you drive me to Hampstead?" He did so, and left me at the top of Tanza Road.'

Mishcon wrote her last two sentences into the statement, at the end of the second paragraph. She signed the statement, and he added the time and the date: 12.30 pm on 12 July 1955. Then Mishcon and Simmons emphasised that it was her duty to let the authorities know the truth, and asked her permission for them to put her statement before the Home Secretary. She replied, offhand: 'If you want to, you can,' and added, as an afterthought, that earlier in the day X had driven her—and Andria—to Epping Forest for firing practice. They decided not to add any more to the statement as time was more important than details, and anyway it did not sound like a point that would be of much help to Ruth's case for a last-minute reprieve.

Ruth herself clearly did not have the slightest idea that she had such a case or that her statement might have any such effect. She took it for granted that the statement had been made purely in order that the truth should be known before she died.

Mishcon telephoned the Home Office to request an immediate interview; then he and Simmons rushed to Whitehall. They asked to see Sir Frank Newsam, the Permanent Under-Secretary, but he was away at the Ascot races. In his absence, the case was being dealt with by Philip (now Sir Philip) Allen, Assistant Under-Secretary of State. He read Ruth's statement and promised that every inquiry would be made to verify the facts. Mishcon asked if that was possible in the few hours left, but Allen would not commit himself; still less to a favourable issue. 'I cannot say that the facts, even if verified, will necessarily justify a reprieve,' he said. Mishcon asked if he could see Lloyd George, but was told that the Home Secretary made it a practice not to see any lawyer involved in a reprieve case.

Reporters were waiting for Mishcon and Simmons when they came out. Mishcon was not only a solicitor but a politician; he had recently completed a year of office as Chairman of the London County Council. It would have been easy to make a dramatic statement, but he did not think that it would help Ruth Ellis: the main thing was to make the Home Secretary realise that this was genuine new evidence, not an artificial campaign organised by someone new to the case. 'It is far better that I say nothing at this stage,' he told the reporters. 'A life is at stake.'

Mishcon and Simmons left the Home Office shortly before 2 pm. Philip Allen instructed an assistant, Miss Baines, to make two telephone calls, one to Ascot, asking for Sir Frank Newsam to be called over the loudspeakers to the telephone, the other to Hampstead Police Station, asking the officer in charge of the case to go immediately to Scotland Yard and to be available for questioning.

Sir Frank Newsam came on the telephone, heard the news, and returned to the Home Office. As Detective Chief Inspector Davies was on the sick list, in bed with a fever, Detective Constable Claiden went to Scotland Yard. He reported to Deputy

Commander Rawlings, who sent him to the Home Office, where he was interviewed by Philip Allen. Allen did not show him Ruth's statement or even say that she had made one. The main points of the interview were later recorded by Detective Inspector Peter Gill, the officer who had taken down Ruth's original statement to the police, and who had been sent for because he was the only senior officer available who had done any work on the case. Gill was not present at the interview but wrote his report with Claiden's help.

> Mr Allen informed the officer that there was a last-minute inquiry concerning the death sentence imposed on Ellis, and asked a number of questions respecting the revolver used by Ellis in the commission of the crime. The officer replied to the effect that it had not been believed that Ellis had had the weapon for three years, but the police could not prove otherwise as they had been unable to trace its origin.
> Mr Allen seemed particularly interested in the possibility that it had been given to her by X . . . DC Claiden observed that it was possible that X had given it to her, but the only evidence of X's possession of guns tended to show that he was not in possession of a revolver a week or two before the tragedy. [*Editors' note: A mistake; Mrs Harris's visit to X's flat occurred nearly three months before the shooting.*] This information had been culled from Mrs Harris, who had seen two pistols in a drawer in X's flat some time before the shooting occurred. It subsequently transpired that these were an air pistol and a starter's pistol, afterwards taken by police from X's flat and identified by Mrs Harris as those she had seen there. Throughout the inquiry police obtained no evidence to connect X with the revolver in question.
> Mr Allen then asked if it was possible that X could have driven Ellis to Hampstead on the night of the shooting, and again he was told that it was possible but nothing had arisen to confirm that suspicion.

There was irony here. Claiden did not mention that X had owned a taxi, presumably because he assumed that Allen already knew; Allen did not ask, because his latest information was Claiden's report of 8 July saying that X had probably never owned a taxi. That report also said that X had disappeared but would be interviewed if he returned: Allen therefore assumed that he was still missing and not likely to be easy to find.

> DC Claiden was then asked by Mr Allen that if Ellis had made a statement to the effect that X had given her the revolver and had

driven her to Hampstead on that night, would it then be possible to charge X with having been an accessory to the crime. Mr Allen was told that, given sufficient evidence, including these two points, it might be possible so to charge X, but the most important consideration must be that X knew that the revolver he had given her was to be used for the purpose of shooting Blakely, and this must be substantiated by evidence other than Ellis's, which would then be that of an accomplice.
The discussion terminated at this point as Mr Allen was due to report to the Home Secretary on this matter. DC Claiden returned to New Scotland Yard, where he joined me. With Deputy Commander Rawlings we then went to see the ACC, where a further discussion took place.

This was interrupted by a telephone call for Richard Jackson, the ACC. He, Gill and Claiden were wanted at the House of Commons, where Philip Allen was waiting for them.

A typescript of a statement made by Ruth Ellis to Mr Victor Mishcon was handed to Mr Jackson and then to me [Gill]. The implications of this statement were discussed at some length, and as a result DC Claiden and I were instructed to trace X and interrogate him in the light of the matters raised therein. We left the House of Commons at about 4.30 pm and began a search for X.

Philip Allen had, of course, assumed all along that a search would be necessary. In point of fact, X had been working in his office as usual for almost all of the four hours that had elapsed since Ruth had signed her statement. Special editions of the evening papers, splashed with headlines about last-minute moves for a reprieve, were already on the streets; they had little news beyond the fact that a new solicitor had spent a long time with Ruth Ellis in Holloway and then rushed to the Home Office. But that could have been enough to induce X to stop work early that afternoon.

We first telephoned his office, and were told that twenty minutes earlier he had left and was believed to be returning to his flat. We went straight there but found that he was not at home. Telephone inquiries of a number of his associates and also places known to be frequented by him were made, but without success . . .

The crowd outside Holloway Prison was already large at tea-time, when Albert Pierrepoint, the hangman, arrived; the crowd grew larger and noisier when children came out of school.

Ruth was still calm, still cheering up her visitors. She told her parents and Granville Neilson about her statement.

Outside the prison, Neilson accepted the help of a scoop-hunting reporter for the last round of his own fight for his sister's life. He went to Mishcon's house, then to the Home Office and the House of Commons, trying hopelessly to get an interview with Gwilym Lloyd George.

That evening, Ruth methodically wrote her last letters.

To a friend:

I am quite happy with the verdict, but not the way the story was told. There is so much that people don't know about.

To George Rogers:

I am quite well—my family have been wonderful. Once again I thank you and your wife. Goodbye.

And finally to Leon Simmons:

Just a line to thank you for coming along with Mr Mishcon this morning.
I have given Mr George Rogers authority to take Clare Andria away for a holiday.
I am now content and satisfied that my affairs will be dealt with satisfactorily. I also ask you to make known the true story regarding Mrs Finlater & her plan to break up David & I—she should feel content, now her plan ended so tragically:
Would you please ask my mother to go to David's grave and put flowers, pink and white carnations. (Ask her to do it for me.)
I would also like to answer David's brother's (newspaper remarks). I admire Derek for defending his brother. I would have been cross with him if he had not. But he said he would have to have more proof than he heard in court before he would believe my story.
My reply to Derek is, I am sorry. I cannot give any more proof than I have.
I did not defend myself. I say a Life for a Life. What more proof can he want?
I have spoken the truth, and I want you to make the truth known for my family and son's sake.
Well, Mr Simmons, the time is 9.30. I am quite well and not worrying about anything.
Thanks once again. RUTH ELLIS

12 JUL 1955

In replying to this letter, please write on the envelope:—

Number 9656 Name ELLIS R

HOLLOWAY. Prison

Dear Mr Simmons,

Just a line to thank you for coming along, with Mr Mishcon this morning.

I have given, Mr George Rogers authority, to take Blore Andrea away for a holiday.

I am now content & satisfied that my affairs will be dealt with satisfactorly

I also, ask you to make known the true story regarding Mrs Findlater & her plan to break up David & I — she should feel content, now her plan ended so tragically.

Would you please ask my mother to go to David's grave, and put flowers Pink & White Carnations. (Ask her to do it for me).

I would, also like to answer David's, brothers, (newspaper remarks)

I admire Derek, for defending, his brother, I would have been cross with him, if he had not. — But he said he would have to have more proof than he heard

No. 243 (21442—3-11-42)

in court, before he would believe my story. —

My reply, to Dereck is,
I am sorry. I cannot give him any more proof, than I have.
I did not defend myself.
I say, a Life for a Life
What more proof can he want?
I have spoken the truth, and I want you to make the truth known, for my family, & sons, sake.
Well, Mr Simmons the time is 9-30, I am quite well, & not worrying about anything.
Thanks Once Again
Ruth Ellis

13-7-55.

Dear Mr Simmons,

Just to let you know, I am still feeling alright. The time is 7 o'clock A.M., — everyone is simply wonderful, in [censored] Holloway.
This is just for you, to remind my family, with the thought, that I did not change my way of thinking at the last moment.
Or break my promise to David's mother.
Well Mr Simmons, I have told you the truth, thats all I can do
Thanks Once Again,
Goodbye
Ruth Ellis

It was a busy night for the Metropolitan Police. The crowd outside Holloway Prison was still large. A section chanted: 'Evans—Bentley—Ellis.'

Detective Inspector Gill and Detective Constable Claiden were still waiting for X to come home.

> We kept observation on his flat until late in the evening, when, on telephoned instructions from Deputy Commander Rawlings, we withdrew, having been unable to see X, who has not yet been again interrogated.

One person who did see X was Granville Neilson. The friendly reporter helped to track him down. Neilson had a faint hope that he might persuade X to come forward and corroborate Ruth's statement. But when Neilson found him, he knew that it was hopeless to ask. X was spending Ruth's last night on earth in bed with another woman.

It did not occur to Neilson to tell the police where X was; their inquiries were so discreet that he did not know that they were looking for him.

Victor Mishcon had no idea that X was missing, but even without that knowledge he did not expect the police to be able to check Ruth's statement properly before nine o'clock next morning. 'I don't know how the most efficient police officers could have done the job in the time,' he said later to Fenton Bresler. 'I had hoped that the very least the Home Secretary would have done would be to postpone the execution, so that proper inquiries could be made.'

Bresler quoted these views to Lord Tenby during their interview some years later. 'The police were, in fact, able to make considerable inquiries,' replied the former Home Secretary, without adding that these inquiries all failed. 'But anyway it made no difference. If anything, if Mrs Ellis's final story was true it made her offence all the greater. Instead of a woman merely acting suddenly on impulse, here you had an actual plot to commit murder, deliberately thought out and conceived with some little care.'

When he said that, Lord Tenby may have learnt about the firing practice in Epping Forest; but he had not heard about it when he decided that Ruth Ellis must still be hanged. All he knew then of her final story was in her written statement, which hardly indicates much deliberate thinking out or careful conception. He gave his real reason for refusing postponement privately at the time: 'If she isn't hanged tomorrow, she never will be.'

Victor Mishcon sat up at home waiting. It was after 2 am when the telephone rang and he was told that there would be no reprieve.

A few hours later, Ruth received the Last Sacrament from the Roman Catholic chaplain at Holloway. Then she wrote a postscript to her letter to Leon Simmons:

> Dear Mr Simmons,
> Just to let you know I am still feeling alright.
> The time is 7 o'clock a.m.—everyone (staff) is simply wonderful in Holloway. This is just for you to console my family with the thought that I did not change my way of thinking at the last moment.
> Or break my promise to David's mother.
> Well, Mr Simmons, I have told you the truth, that's all I can do.
> Thanks once again.
> Goodbye. RUTH ELLIS

'Hanging criminals is the favourite sport of the English,' wrote a French visitor, B. L. de Muralt, in 1694.

In 1955, shortly before 9 am on 13 July, the headmaster of a school in Middlesex saw four of his boys standing still on the playground. One held a watch. 'Only four more minutes,' the child said. 'One . . . two . . . three . . . four—she's had it, boys!'

She had had it. Granville Neilson, in a newspaper office, saw the news come through on the tickertape. She had had it. It said so, more primly, in the official notice put up outside Holloway Prison. A crowd of about a thousand surged forward to read the notice; a man lifted up his small daughter so that she could see.

Ruth Ellis was dead, and in a school near the prison the children were in a ferment. 'Some claim to have seen the execution from their windows, others spoke with fascinated horror of the technique of hanging a female,' said one of the teachers. 'Not only was Ruth Ellis hanged today, hundreds of children were a little corrupted.'

The execution had been carried out expeditiously and without a hitch, in the officially approved formula, and Albert Pierrepoint could collect his small fee and go back to his pub, Help the Poor Struggler.

The Home Office pathologist, Dr Keith Simpson, examined the body, found that the deceased was 'a healthy subject at the time of death', and gave the cause of death as 'injuries to the central nervous system consequent upon judicial hanging'. He recorded the contents of her stomach as 'small food residue, and odour of brandy'. Later, a Member of Parliament, a medical practitioner himself, complained to the Home Office about the extensiveness of the necropsy; he said that the Coroner ought not to have ordered a full post-mortem examination merely to establish that the hanging had proved fatal.

The inquest was conducted by Mr J. Milner-Helme, HM Coroner for the City of London. Although Davies and Claiden attended to identify the body, the Coroner sent for Granville Neilson to do this. Neilson recalls that his sister was laid out on boards and trestles in the open air, under an arch close to the execution shed; there were two candles and a crucifix at the head. 'I did not see any marks on her neck. I remember that I looked at her face and said: "She still looks beautiful, doesn't she?" '

Later, the Home Office received a complaint from another MP, who said it was the custom to call police officers to identify the body, to spare a relative or friend from this harrowing experience. (A few words in the report of the 1949–53 Royal Commission suggest that it could be extremely harrowing—'hanging leaves the body with the neck elongated'—but happily Granville Neilson did not notice.) The Home Office supported this complaint when passing it to Mr Milner-Helme, who replied that he had called the deceased's brother because he felt that this was safer—'for it is possible, though very unlikely, that the deceased had been living under an assumed name ever since before she first came into contact with the police'. Mr Milner-Helme, who gave us this information shortly before his death in February 1973, added the comment: 'I understand that it *is* the practice of coroners to call the police to identify the body of the deceased in an inquest after execution. Indeed, this case was the only one in which I did not follow the practice. For I did not think earlier of the remote risk involved in calling the police. The Home Office, of course, had no authority to dictate to coroners.'

Chief Inspector Davies wrote his final report on the case two days later, on Thursday, 15 July; with it he enclosed the statement made by X about his taxi almost a week earlier, on 9 July. 'X was very closely interrogated regarding the fact that he owned a taxi cab,' Davies reported, 'and as to his movements on the evening of 10 April 1955 . . . At the same time I subjected him to further questioning regarding the origin of the gun used by Mrs Ellis, but he maintained he had not given it to her and had never seen this revolver.' (There was nothing to that effect in X's statement.)

Davies's report was sent to the ACC. It was not sent to the Home Office, and the Home Office never asked if X had been found and questioned. The police did not check the date when X had disposed of the taxi, and they made no further attempt to see X and ask him about Ruth's statement to Victor Mishcon. *Rigor mortis* had set in regarding the case.

But, of course, many persons still thought that Ruth Ellis ought not to have been hanged.

One was Duncan Webb, the crime reporter of *The People*, who carried out an investigation of his own. He talked to Ruth's relatives, including her son, Andria, who had never been interviewed by either the police or the defence. Webb reported that the boy had given him more details about how he and his mother had spent Easter Sunday. Some time during that day, he said, X had driven Ruth and Andria to Tanza Road, Hampstead, and then to Penn. Ruth had sent Andria to see if Blakely's car was outside his flat, but it was not. On the way back, he had heard them talking about a gun; he heard Ruth say that she wanted a gun, and X say that he could provide one.

That was the story published by Duncan Webb six months after Ruth's execution. Webb could not suggest a motive for the trip, but then he did not know that Blakely had driven the Findlaters' nanny to Victoria Station. The most reasonable theory seems to be that Ruth went to Tanza Road to resume her watch on the house. She either had found Blakely's car gone or had seen him drive off with the nanny and no one else, a sight that would have inflamed her jealousy to a murderous pitch. X would not have had much chance to follow the fast-driving Blakely, and it would have been logical for Ruth to drive to Penn to see if he had taken the girl to his flat. Finding no car at Penn, X could have driven Ruth and Andria back to London to collect the gun and perhaps look again for Blakely's car in Tanza Road on their way to the firing practice in Epping Forest.

Ruth and Andria evidently went after this to Cussen's flat, for he took them back to Egerton Gardens at about seven o'clock. That would still have given her time to go to X's flat and drink Pernod before being driven to Hampstead to shoot Blakely at 9.15 pm.

Ruth's loyalty to X after her arrest was so remarkable that Duncan Webb deduced that they had made a pact: in return for her silence he promised to provide financially for Andria when she was dead. Webb guessed that she named X at the end because he was failing to keep his side of the bargain. That part is clearly nonsense, and Granville Neilson is sure that there was no pact at all apart from the obvious one: her silence in return for X's help regarding the gun and the ride to Hampstead.

After the execution, critical comments appeared in two influential weekly journals, *The Economist* and *The Spectator*, and the death penalty was roundly attacked on 23 July in *The Lancet*, the leading organ of the medical profession (*see Appendix 3*).

'Undoubtedly the Ruth Ellis case played a large part in developing public opinion against capital punishment,' recalls Anthony Wedgwood Benn, one of the MPs who were launching a new attempt to get the law changed.

A month after the execution, the National Campaign for the Abolition of Capital Punishment was publicly launched. The campaign was started by Victor Gollancz, Canon John Collins and Arthur Koestler at Gollancz's country house in the summer of 1955. 'As far as I can remember,' Koestler says, 'that visit took place before the execution of Ruth Ellis, and in so far as I am concerned it was not her case which motivated the launching of the campaign. But quite obviously the public revulsion against that execution provided the emotional background for the campaign in its early stages.'

Seven months after Ruth Ellis was hanged, the Commons, on a free vote, resolved 'that this House believes that the death penalty no longer accords with the needs or the true interests of a civilised society', and a Bill to abolish it was passed through all its stages. Like the 1948 Bill, it was rejected by the Lords. But no one was hanged in 1956; all murderers were routinely reprieved. Then, in March 1957, the Homicide Act was passed, giving the executioner a new but limited lease of life: hanging was reserved for certain kinds of murder, including any murder by shooting. 'If Ruth Ellis had used a hatchet, she would have been all right under this Bill, but not if she used a revolver,' complained one MP during the debate; but she would probably have been all right anyway, as the Act admitted into England the Scottish defence of diminished responsibility. In at least two cases of a *crime passionel*—Fantle in 1958 and Holford in 1962—this defence was successfully invoked to reduce the charge to manslaughter, and in each case the punishment was three years' imprisonment.

Ruth Ellis was buried within the walls of Holloway Prison; it was the custom not to hand over the bodies of hanged persons to their relatives, because of the elongation of the neck. But fifteen years later, some rebuilding was done at the prison, and the remains of all the executed women were disturbed. Ruth's body was the most recent as she was the last woman to be hanged in England. The authorities asked her son if he would like her remains to be cremated or re-interred, and he chose a reburial at St Mary's, Amersham. And there she lies now, under the name of Ruth Hornby, only a couple of miles or so from David Blakely's grave at Penn.

The small churchyard of St Mary's should be a place of pilgrimage for those who retain an ardent belief that no murderer should be hanged, for there is little doubt that the execution of Ruth Ellis played a major part in bringing about the abolition of capital punishment.

LEADING DATES

1926	October	9	Ruth Neilson born at 74 West Parade, Rhyl.
1929	June	17	David Blakely born at Oakdale Nursing Home, Sheffield. (Parents' address: 203 School Road, Crookes, Sheffield.)
1944	September		Ruth Neilson gives birth to illegitimate son, Clare Andria Neilson.
1950	November	8	Ruth Neilson marries George Ellis.
1951	October		Georgina Ellis born.
	November		George Ellis refused order to file petition for divorce.
1953	? November		David Blakely starts living with Ruth Ellis.
1954	May	26	George Ellis files petition for divorce.
1955	January	14	Decree nisi awarded to George Ellis.
	February	25	Decree nisi made absolute.
	March	28	Ruth Ellis suffers a miscarriage.
	April	10	David Blakely shot dead. Ruth Ellis arrested.
		11	Ruth Ellis charged with murder and remanded in custody.
		28	Committal proceedings at Hampstead Magistrates' Court.
	May	11	Ruth Ellis arraigned at the Central Criminal Court before Mr Justice Barrie. Case put over to next session.
	June	20	Trial begins.
		21	Trial ends. Ruth Ellis sentenced to death.
		22	Announcement by defence solicitors that Ruth Ellis will not appeal.
	July	11	Home Secretary declines to advise a reprieve.
		12	Ruth Ellis makes written statement naming her accomplice.
		13	Ruth Ellis hanged at Holloway Prison.

	August		Launching of the National Campaign for the Abolition of Capital Punishment.
1956	February		Bill to abolish death penalty passed by House of Commons.
	March		Same Bill rejected by House of Lords.
1957	March		Homicide Act, restricting death penalty and admitting defence of diminished responsibility (eg in cases of *crime passionel*).
1965	November		Death penalty suspended for five years.
1969	December		Death penalty abolished.
1971	April	1	Remains of Ruth Ellis re-buried at St Mary's, Amersham.

Page 81 Ruth Ellis

Page 82 (*left*) Goodwood Court

(*right*) Egerton Gardens (No 44 is the third entrance from the left)

Page 83 Mr and Mrs Anthony Findlater, Ruth Ellis, David Blakely

le match

ELLE A PLAIDE COUPABLE PAR AMOUR

Ruth Ellis, 28 ans, ancien mannequin, était l'hôtesse d'un club de Kensington. Elle est mère de deux enfants. C'est par jalousie qu'elle abattit le coureur automobiliste David Blakely. Elle avait d'abord refusé de signer son recours en grâce.

Pages 84 and 85 The first two pages of a feature or

e la vie

Six balles tirées " avec l'intention de donner la mort " l'ont conduite dans la cellule des condamnées à la peine capitale. Mais toute l'Angleterre s'est émue devant l'inflexibilité de sa justice qui n'admet pas l'excuse de la passion.

UTH ELLIS
AS DE CONSCIENCE
E L'ANGLETERRE

› l'huissier à chaine d'argent déposa sur son bureau le dossier vert '« affaire Ruth Ellis », l'imperturbable major Gwilym Lloyd George, du célèbre homme politique, ne put maitriser un tressaillement de e. Comme pour chasser des pensées inopportunes, il passa la main ront, puis demanda à n'être dérangé sous aucun prétexte.
t, l'histoire était banale, mais le destin l'avait transformée en une bombe. Pour la première fois depuis des siècles une brèche s'ouvrait xpugnable citadelle de la justice anglaise. Cette bombe, il appartenait au major, Home secretary de Sa Majesté, d'y mettre ou non le feu. S'il recommandait à la Reine de rejeter le recours en grâce formulé par Ruth Ellis, vingt-huit ans, condamnée pour un meurtre passionnel à être pendue, la vieille machine judiciaire britannique continuerait à fonctionner sur le rythme de la tradition. Si, au contraire, il proposait sa grâce, le premier pas, le plus dur, serait fait dans la voie de réformes qui bouleverseraient le système actuel. En ne pendant pas Ruth Ellis, l'Angleterre désavouerait sa législation et prendrait officieusement en considération le drame passionnel.

(*Suite page* 80.)

IL LUI PREFERAIT LES COURSES

David Blakely, 25 ans, fils de famille, n'avait qu'une passion, les courses. Il avait construit lui-même sa voiture Emperor (à g.). C'est le dimanche de Pâques qu'il a été tué. Il avait l'intention de participer aux 24 Heures du Mans.

JACQUES LE BAILLY

ıse published in *Paris Match*, 23 and 30 July 1955

Page 86 (*left*) 29 Tanza Road

(*right*) The Magdala

Page 87 Desmond Cussen

Page 88 People rushing to see the Execution Notice outside Holloway Prison on the morning of 13 July 1955

THE TRIAL

within the

CENTRAL CRIMINAL COURT,
OLD BAILEY, LONDON

Monday, 20 June 1955,
and succeeding day

BEFORE

MR JUSTICE HAVERS
(and a jury)

THE QUEEN

against

RUTH ELLIS

MR CHRISTMAS HUMPHREYS, MR MERVYN GRIFFITH-JONES, and MISS JEAN SOUTHWORTH appeared on behalf of the Crown

(Instructed by the Director of Public Prosecutions)

MR MELFORD STEVENSON, QC, MR SEBAG SHAW, and MR PETER RAWLINSON appeared on behalf of the accused

(Instructed by Messrs. Cardew-Smith & Ross, London)

FIRST DAY

Monday, 20 June 1955

THE CLERK OF THE COURT: Ruth Ellis, you are charged that on 10 April last you murdered David Moffet Drummond Blakely. How say you, are you guilty or not guilty?

THE PRISONER: Not guilty.

A jury of ten men and two women was empanelled and sworn.

THE CLERK: Members of the jury, the prisoner at the Bar, Ruth Ellis, is charged with the murder of David Blakely on 10 April last. To this indictment she has pleaded not guilty, and it is your charge to say, having heard the evidence, whether she be guilty or not.

MR HUMPHREYS *opened the case on behalf of the Crown:*

Mrs Ellis is a woman of twenty-eight, divorced, and the story which you are going to hear outlined is this: that in 1954 and 1955 she was having simultaneous love affairs with two men, one of whom was the deceased and the other a man called Cussen, whom I shall call before you.

It would seem that, lately, Blakely, the deceased man, was trying to break off the connection, and that the accused woman was angry at the thought that he should leave her, even though she had another lover at the time. She therefore took a gun which she knew to be loaded, which she put in her bag. She says in a statement which she signed: 'When I put the gun in my bag, I intended to find David and shoot him.' She found David and she shot him dead by emptying that revolver at him, four bullets going into his body, one hitting a bystander in the hand, and the sixth going we know not where.

That, in a very few words, is the case for the Crown, and nothing else I say to you, in however much detail, will add to the stark simplicity of that story.

After reading extracts from the prisoner's statement to the police [see page 103], MR HUMPHREYS *continued:*

In 1953 Mrs Ellis was a hostess at the Little Club in Knightsbridge. She lived in a flat over it. There she met Blakely, and about the end of 1953 she began to live with him.

In the summer of 1954 she began to have an affair at the same time with a man called Cussen. In December 1954 she left the Little Club and went to live with Cussen at his flat in Goodwood Court, Devonshire Street. She continued, however, to see

Blakely. It would seem, therefore, that for the remaining few months of the story, she was living in that sense with both men.

Early this year she [*sic; it was Blakely who telephoned Findlater asking to be rescued from Ruth Ellis*] telephoned a man called Findlater, a friend of Blakely's, who had a flat in Tanza Road, Hampstead. As a consequence, Findlater and a man called Gunnell went to Cussen's flat, where Ellis was living. It would seem that she was complaining that Blakely was trying to leave her, and she was trying to stop him going.

On 9 February she went to live in a bed-sitting-room at 44 Egerton Gardens, South Kensington. She lived there with Blakely, who was known as Mr Ellis. While there, she was visited by Cussen.

But let me tell you at once, as no doubt his Lordship will echo, that you are not here in the least concerned with adultery or any sexual misconduct. You are not trying for immorality but for murder, and the only importance of these movements between her and these various men is that it will help you to see the frame of mind she was in when she did what it cannot be denied in fact she did.

Over the Easter weekend, Blakely went to stay with Mr Findlater at his home in Tanza Road. It would seem that, at this time, Blakely was trying to part from Mrs Ellis and had arranged the weekend visit for that purpose.

Mrs Ellis spent Good Friday with Mr Cussen. She telephoned Mr Findlater in the evening and asked if Blakely was with him. Mr Findlater, not telling the truth, said he was not. At about midnight Mrs Ellis telephoned Mr Cussen, her alternative lover, and he drove her to Hampstead, dropping her at the corner of Tanza Road. It would seem that, some time after that, at about 1 am, Blakely, who was sleeping on a sofa, and Findlater were awakened by noises outside. Mrs Ellis was hammering in the windows of Blakely's car and ringing the doorbell repeatedly. The police were called, but Blakely and Findlater were again awakened, at about 3 am, by Mrs Ellis hitting the windows of the car, and for a second time the police were called to send her away. On the following day, the Saturday, Mrs Ellis telephoned the Findlaters' flat, but the receiver was hung up on her.

Well, by this time you have a fairly clear idea of the attitude of the man who was staying at the Findlaters' instead of spending the weekend with Mrs Ellis.

On Sunday—the all-important day—Findlater, Blakely and others held a party at the flat in Tanza Road, and at about 8.45 pm Blakely and his friend Mr Gunnell went about three-quarters of a mile to a public-house, the Magdala, to buy some more beer.

Matters then rapidly moved to a climax. There was in the public-house a Police Constable Thompson, who was off duty and in plain clothes. At about nine o'clock, he will tell you, he saw Mrs Ellis looking through the public-house windows a few minutes after Blakely and Gunnell had entered. At about 9.15 Blakely and Gunnell left the Magdala, carrying the beer they had bought. Gunnell went to one side of their car. Then he heard two shots and someone running. Rushing round to the other side of the car, he heard Blakely calling him, and saw his friend lying on his stomach on the ground. Between Blakely and a wall stood Mrs Ellis with a gun in her hand. It was pointed at Blakely's back.

She fired at him several times more. Gunnell ran to pick up his friend, and Ellis came up to him and told him: 'Now go and call the police.' Blakely was lying face downwards on the pavement, groaning.

An ambulance took Blakely to hospital, but he died on arrival. The cause of death was shock and serious haemorrhage from the wounds. He had three definite bullet wounds—one above the left hip, one in the left shoulder blade, one in the right leg—and a possible fourth: there was a graze in the left arm which could have been caused by a bullet. A fifth bullet fired from the gun hit a Mrs Yule, who was passing at the time, in the hand.

At 11.30 that night, Mrs Ellis was seen by Detective Superintendent Crawford at Hampstead Police Station. He said to her: 'I have seen the dead body of David Blakely at Hampstead Mortuary. I understand you know something about it.' He cautioned her, and her reply was: 'I am guilty. I am rather confused. It all started about two years ago. When I met David. At the Little Club. In Knightsbridge.' Mrs Ellis then elected to make a statement. The only comment I would make upon that statement . . . is that she never mentions Mr Cussen from start to end.

MR HUMPHREYS *read extracts from the statement, then ended his speech:*

Members of the jury, there in its stark simplicity is the case for the Crown, and whatever be the background and whatever may have been in her mind when she took that gun, if you have no doubt that she took that gun with the sole purpose of finding and shooting David Blakely and that she then shot him dead, in my submission to you, subject to his Lordship's ruling in law, the only verdict is wilful murder. If, during the trial, any matters arise which enable you, under his Lordship's direction, to find some lesser verdict, then you will so do.

Now, with the assistance of my learned friends, I will call the evidence before you.

EVIDENCE FOR THE PROSECUTION

POLICE CONSTABLE PHILIP BANYARD *of 'S' Division of the Metropolitan Police proved a plan he had prepared of the area of the shooting.* (*No cross-examination.*)

DETECTIVE CONSTABLE THOMAS MACMACKEN *of the Photographic Department, New Scotland Yard, testified as to photographs he had taken of the body of David Blakely at Hampstead Mortuary.* (*No cross-examination.*)

MRS JOAN ADA WINSTANLEY, *formerly the housekeeper at* 44 *Egerton Gardens, Kensington, said that on* 18 *February* 1955 *Mrs Ellis called at the house and said that she wished to reserve a room for herself and her husband; the following day, she moved in. Mrs Winstanley later saw a man at the house who was referred to as Mr Ellis and called David by Mrs Ellis.* (*No cross-examination.*)

DESMOND EDWARD CUSSEN, *living at Goodwood Court, Devonshire Street, Marylebone, examined by* MR HUMPHREYS: I knew Blakely for about three years. I first met Mrs Ellis about two years ago, when she was manageress of the Little Club, Knightsbridge, of which Blakely was a member. She became a close friend of Blakely's, and lived with him. In October 1953 I, too, became a close friend of hers.

You will not mind if we use plain words. Were you her lover at some time?—For a short time.

When was that?—About June 1954.

What was Blakely's position? Had he broken with her? Was he still seeing her?—He was away for about a week.

When he came back, what was the position?—He carried on seeing her and being very friendly.

Did she at some time live with you?—She left the Little Club at the end of December 1954 and came to stay at my flat.

And what was her attitude to Blakely?—It had not changed.

How long did she live at your flat?—About two months. Then she went to Egerton Gardens.

Do you know in what circumstances she was living there?—I understand that Blakely stayed there with her.

Did you see her at Egerton Gardens?—(*Pause.*) Yes.

Did she continue to see you at your flat?—(*Pause.*) Yes.

In answer to further questions, the witness stated that on Good Friday, 1955, *Mrs Ellis wanted to go to Mr Findlater's flat; he understood that Blakely had promised to drive her there. Blakely did not do so, and he (the witness) took her to Tanza Road, Hampstead, at about* 12.30 *the following morning. He waited about three-quarters of an hour for her; when she came back she said that she had pushed in the window of Blakely's car and the police had been called.*

On Sunday, 10 April, did she and her son spend most of the day with you at your flat?—Yes.

How old was the boy?—Ten.

That evening, did you drive her back to Egerton Gardens?—Yes.

About what time?—About 7.30.

At 7.30 on the Sunday night: and that is the last you saw of her?—Yes.

Cross-examined by MR STEVENSON:

You have told the jury that you and this young woman were lovers for a short time in June 1954. Is that right?—Yes.

And that was the time when Blakely was away, was it not—at the Le Mans race in France?—Yes.

Were you very much in love with this young woman?—I was terribly fond of her at the time, yes.

Did she tell you from time to time that she would like to get away from Blakely, but could not, or words to that effect?—Yes.

And at that time did she repeatedly go back to him?—Yes.

At a time when you were begging her to marry you if she could?—Yes.

Have you ever seen any marks or bruises on her?—Yes.

How often?—On several occasions.

How recently before Easter had you seen marks of that kind?—On one occasion when I was taking her to a dance.

When was that?—25 February.

MR JUSTICE HAVERS: Of this year?—Yes, my Lord.

'When I was taking her to a dance'?—Yes.

MR STEVENSON: Did you help to disguise bruises on her shoulders?—Yes.

Were they bad bruises?—Yes, and they required quite heavy make-up, too.

I do not want to press you for details, but how often have you seen that sort of mark on her?—It must be on half-a-dozen occasions.

Did you on one occasion take her to the Middlesex Hospital?—Yes, I did.

Why was that?—She came back when she was staying at my flat, and when I arrived back I found her in a very bad condition.

In what respect?—She had definitely been very badly bruised all over the body.

Did she receive treatment for that condition at Middlesex Hospital?—Yes.

ANTHONY SEATON FINDLATER, *living at 29 Tanza Road, Hampstead, examined by* MR HUMPHREYS: On 9 January this year I went to a flat in Marylebone with Blakely and another friend, Clive Gunnell. Ruth Ellis was there. Blakely asked me if I could assist him to leave her. This was said in her presence. I cannot remember her exact words, but she was rather sarcastic about him needing some help to leave her. The meeting ended with Blakely going off by himself.

At about this time, Blakely and I were building a racing car which was kept at Rex Place, Mayfair.

Early in April this year I went with Blakely and Ruth Ellis to the motor races at Chester; she and Blakely were living together as husband and wife.

On Good Friday evening Mrs Ellis rang me at home to ask if Blakely was with me. He had arranged to spend the holiday with me, and was there in the flat, but he asked me to tell Mrs Ellis he was not. I was awakened at about 2 am by Blakely because Mrs

Ellis was ringing the doorbell and pushing in the windows of his car; I telephoned the police and she went away. Later I was awakened again by Blakely as the same thing was happening; again I sent for the police.

On Saturday morning the damage to the windows of the car was repaired by Blakely and myself at Rex Place, and Mrs Ellis telephoned while we were there.

I had a few friends at my flat on Easter Sunday, and during the evening Blakely and Clive Gunnell left to get some more beer. That was the last I saw of Blakely.

Cross-examined by MR STEVENSON:

You for some time received £10 a week, did you not, from Blakely for your services in connection with a racing motor car which he was building?—Yes, that is right.

Was that at that time your sole source of income?—Yes, it was.

When you saw Blakely and Mrs Ellis at the flat in Marylebone, had Blakely asked you to go there?—Yes.

And asked you to go there because he wanted your help, is that right?—Yes, he wanted my help.

When Mrs Ellis telephoned your home on Good Friday, you lied when you said that David Blakely was not there?—Yes.

It was the night of Good Friday and Easter Saturday that she pushed in the windows of Blakely's car?—Yes, that is right.

When I say 'pushed in', she put such pressure on them, or some of them, that they came out of their rubber seating. Is that right?—Yes, that is right.

You know something about motor cars, I suppose?—Yes.

Would it be right to say that, in order to push such windows out of their rubber seatings, you would have to exert great pressure?—Not a great pressure, I think. I think a good sort of thump, or something like that, would push them out. It is not great pressure.

At any rate, how many windows did she push out that night?—One side one and two back ones, I think.

Was it quite plain when you spoke to her on the telephone that she was in a desperate state of emotion?—No.

What?—I said no.

Do you mean she was quite calm? Do you really mean that?—It was just a telephone conversation. She rang me up, as she had done hundreds of times, and asked if I knew where David was. It was just a telephone conversation.

I know it was just a telephone conversation. Just bear in mind what she said and the way she said it and the fact that she afterwards pushed out those windows. Did you observe no indication of her being a very desperate woman at that time?—No.

Never mind about the word 'desperate'. Was it obvious to you that she was in a state of considerable emotional disturbance?—Well, I did not get that impression over the 'phone. She might have been.

Perhaps you are not very good at judging that sort of thing on the telephone. Are you?—I think so.

At the time of these events, did you have in your household a young woman of eighteen or nineteen who looked after your child?—Yes.

On the evening of Easter Saturday, was there a Rolls-Royce outside your house?—Yes.

Did you and Blakely go out with the young woman and get into the car?—I cannot remember.

You cannot remember?—No.

As you were walking down the steps of 29 Tanza Road, did not Blakely say to the young woman: 'Let me put my arm around you for support'?—I do not remember.

Did you see this young woman, the nanny, and Blakely outside, pointing to the windows of the car that had been repaired?—No.

Your wife was in the flat all through the weekend, was not she?—Yes.

Re-examined by MR HUMPHREYS:

You will appreciate what is being suggested: that there is some reason for Ruth Ellis being jealous of some new woman being on the stage?—I did not even know that Mrs Ellis knew we had a nanny. She knew we had one, but this was quite a new one.

What my friend is putting is that Ruth Ellis, in hanging about, might have seen Blakely in the presence of an entirely new young woman. I am sure you will help us if you can, if you were fooling about or anything of that sort. Was there any incident with a young woman outside the house that you can remember?—No.

BERTRAM CLIVE GUNNELL, *a car salesman, examined by* MR HUMPHREYS: I knew David Blakely for five years, and have known

Mr Findlater for seven years, and Ruth Ellis for six months; it was David who introduced me to Mrs Ellis.

I recall an interview at a flat in Marylebone in January this year at which David asked Findlater and me to take him away from Mrs Ellis.

On Easter Sunday I went to Findlater's flat for a party; we were drinking beer and playing the gramophone. At about a quarter to nine, the beer ran out, and Blakely and I left to go to the Magdala public house to fetch more. We stayed there ten or fifteen minutes, leaving Blakely's Vanguard parked outside.

I came out first, carrying a bottle. I went round to the passenger seat, but the door was locked, so I had to wait for David Blakely. While I was waiting, I heard two bangs and a shout of 'Clive'. I went round the back of the car and saw David lying on the ground. Mrs Ellis was firing a gun into his back. I ran to Blakely and heard Mrs Ellis say: 'Now call the police.'

(*No cross-examination.*)

LEWIS CHARLES NICKOLLS, *Director of the Metropolitan Police Laboratory, New Scotland Yard, examined by* MR HUMPHREYS: I am a Master of Science and a Fellow of the Royal Institute of Chemistry. On 12 April 1955 I received from Chief Inspector Davies and Detective Constable Claiden, both of 'S' Division, Hampstead:

1. One .38 Smith & Wesson revolver containing six cartridge cases.
2. Two spent bullets.
3. One sample of blood from the deceased, David Blakely.
4. Two samples of stomach contents from the deceased.
5. A quantity of capsules of one type, and one capsule of another; these were found in the deceased's possession.
6. Scrapings of bloodstains from the rear of a Vanguard car, registration number OPH 615.

I found that the blood (3) contained 106 milligrammes of alcohol per 100 millilitres, indicating the consumption of the equivalent of approximately four pints of beer, or a fluid ounce of spirits. This blood is of group A.

The stomach contents (4) contained the remains of a comparatively recently consumed meal.

All but one of the capsules (5) are of amyl nitrate, and are used in cases of heart disease to cause dilation of the veins, and also in the relief of asthma. The single capsule is a spansule of amphetamine sulphate; a spansule contains a large number of pellets which dissolve at varying rates in the intestinal juices so that medication is obtained over a period of some hours.

The blood (6) is human blood of group A.

The revolver (1) was in working order. The barrel was foul and consistent with having been recently fired, otherwise the revolver was in clean condition and was oily. The two bullets (2) are similar bullets from the .38 revolver ammunition. They have both been fired from a Smith & Wesson revolver, and comparison of these bullets with bullets fired in the laboratory from the revolver (1) shows a similarity of patterns which indicates that the bullets (2) have been fired from this revolver.

MR HUMPHREYS: Can you help us at all as to the distance from the body at which any of the bullets had been fired in respect of the wounds found in the body?—Yes. I examined the clothing of the deceased man, and I found that on the left shoulder at the back of the jacket there was a bullet hole. This had been fired at a distance of less than three inches.

Will you identify the garment?—(*Exhibit—a dark grey jacket—produced to the witness.*) Yes. (*Exhibit passed to the jury.*)

MR JUSTICE HAVERS: Why do you say that?—That is because of the circle of powder-fouling round the hole. The others are all fired from a distance.

A powder-fouling?—Yes. There is a circular powder residue. All the other shots had been fired at a distance.

(*No cross-examination.*)

POLICE CONSTABLE ALAN THOMPSON *of 'L' Division of the Metropolitan Police:* On the night of Easter Sunday I was off duty and in plain clothes. At approximately 9.15 I was in the saloon bar of the Magdala public-house, South End Road, Hampstead, and I noticed a blonde woman wearing spectacles looking into the bar through a rippled-glass window near the door; I could not see her face clearly as she was very close to the glass, but I believe she was the accused. About five minutes later, I heard several explosions from close at hand. I ran out into the street and saw a man lying on his left cheek, close to a Vanguard motor-car which was parked outside the Magdala; he was moaning and bleeding from the mouth. The accused was standing with her back to the wall of the public-house. She was holding a revolver. She told me to telephone the police. I said that I was a police officer, and took the fire-arm from her. I told her that I was detaining her, and gave her the required caution, to which she said nothing. Mr Clive Gunnell informed me that he was a friend of the wounded man, whose name was David Blakely. A few minutes later, an ambulance arrived, and Mr Blakely was taken to New End Hospital; Mr Gunnell went with the ambulance. I took Mrs Ellis to Hampstead Police Station in Rosslyn Hill, arriving there at about 10 pm.

(*No cross-examination.*)

MRS GLADYS KENSINGTON YULE, *living at 24 Parliament Hill, Hampstead Heath, N.W.3, stated that she and her husband left home at about nine o'clock on the night of Easter Sunday, intending to have a drink at the Magdala. As they reached the corner of Parliament Hill and South End Road, there was a commotion outside the public-house, and shots were fired. The witness felt a searing pain in her right hand, causing her to drop the hand-bag which she was holding; she saw that the hand was bleeding. A taxi-cab came along, and she and her husband got in and were driven to Hampstead General Hospital, where she was detained for treatment for a bullet wound through the base of her thumb; the bullet had passed through her hand, fracturing the first metacarpal bone.*

(*No cross-examination.*)

DR ALBERT CHARLES HUNT, *pathologist at The London Hospital Medical College, testified that he performed a post-mortem examination of David Blakely at 9.30 on the morning of Easter Monday, 11 April. There was an entry wound of a bullet in the lower part of the back, to the right, with a track leading from this through the abdominal cavity, perforating the intestine and liver and ending in an exit wound below the left shoulder blade. A second track ran upwards through the chest, perforating the left lung, the aorta and the windpipe, and the bullet was lodged in the deep muscles of the right of the tongue; this bullet was removed and later handed to Detective Constable Claiden. There was another injury just above the outer part of the left hip bone, penetrating the skin and underlying fat only, and with an exit wound quite close to that. There was also a shallow mark on the inner side of the left forearm. The witness could not be sure whether these last two injuries were caused by one bullet or by two. It was his opinion that the cause of death was shock and haemorrhage due to gunshot wounds.*

(*No cross-examination.*)

DETECTIVE CONSTABLE GEORGE CLAIDEN *of 'S' Division of the Metropolitan Police testified that he received a .38 spent bullet from the previous witness, and that he handed this, and other items, to Mr L. C. Nickolls.* (*No cross-examination.*)

DETECTIVE CHIEF INSPECTOR LESLIE DAVIES *of 'S' Division of the Metropolitan Police, examined by* MR HUMPHREYS: At 11.30 pm on Easter Sunday, 10 April, at Hampstead Police Station, the defendant was interviewed by Detective Superintendent Leonard Crawford, Detective Inspector Peter Gill, and myself.

What did Mr Crawford say to her at that time?—Mr Crawford said: 'I have just seen the dead body of David Blakely at Hampstead Mortuary. I understand that you know something about it,' and he cautioned her.

Just tell the jury what that means.—He said to her: 'You are not obliged to say anything at all about this unless you wish to do so, but whatever you say will be taken down in writing and may be given in evidence.'

What did she say?—She said: 'I am guilty. I am rather confused,' and then she—

Just a moment. Did you form any impression of her emotional condition at that time?—I did. I was most impressed by the fact that she seemed very composed.

I did ask you about her emotional condition. What about her mental condition when she said she was confused?—There was no sign of confusion in her manner, or attitude, at all.

After saying: 'I am guilty. I am rather confused,' did she say anything else?—She continued: 'It all started about two years ago. When I met David. At the Little Club. In Knightsbridge.'

And then what happened?—Mr Crawford stopped her and asked: 'Would you like this to be written down?'

What was her reply?—'Yes.'

Please go on.—She signed another caution, and made the following statement, which was taken down by Detective Inspector Gill:

I understand what has been said. I am guilty. I am rather confused.

About two years ago I met David Blakely when I was manageress of the Little Club, Knightbridge; my flat was above that. I had known him for about a fortnight when he started to live with me, and has done so continuously until last year, when he went away to Le Mans for about three weeks, motor racing. He came back to me and remained living with me until Good Friday morning.

He left me about ten o'clock am and promised to be back by 8 pm to take me out. I waited until half-past nine and he had not 'phoned, although he always had done in the past. I was rather worried at that stage as he had had trouble with his racing car and had been drinking.

I rang some friends of his named Findlater at Hampstead, but they told me he was not there, although David had told me he was visiting them. I was speaking to Findlater, and I asked if David was all right. He laughed and said: 'Oh, yes, he's all right.' I did not believe he was not there, and I took a taxi to Hampstead, where I saw David's car outside Findlater's flat at 28 [*sic*] Tanza Road. I then telephoned from nearby, and when my voice was recognised they hung up on me.

I went to the flat and continually rang the door-bell, but they would not answer. I became very furious and went to David's car, which was still standing there, and pushed in three of the side windows. The noise I made must have aroused the Findlaters, as the police came along and spoke to me. Mr Findlater came out of his flat, and the police also spoke to him.

David did not come home on Saturday, and at nine o'clock this morning (Sunday) I 'phoned the Findlaters again, and Mr Findlater answered. I said to him: 'I hope you are having an enjoyable holiday,' and was about to say: 'because you have ruined mine,' and he banged the receiver down.

I waited all day today (Sunday) for David to 'phone, but he did not do so. About eight o'clock this evening (Sunday) I put my son Andria to bed. I then took a gun which I had hidden, and put it in my handbag. This gun was given to me about three years ago in a club by a man whose name I do not remember. It was security for money, but I accepted it as a curiosity. I did not know it was loaded when it was given to me, but I knew next morning when I looked at it. When I put the gun in my bag I intended to find David and shoot him.

I took a taxi to Tanza Road, and as I arrived, David's car drove away from Findlater's address. I dismissed the taxi and walked back down the road to the nearest pub, where I saw David's car outside. I waited outside until he came out with a friend I know as Clive. David went to his car door to open it. I was a little way away from him. He turned and saw me and then turned away from me, and I took the gun from my bag and I shot him. He turned round and ran a few steps round the car. I thought I had missed him, so I fired again. He was still running, and I fired the third shot. I don't remember firing any more, but I must have done. I remember then he was lying on the footway and I was standing beside him. He was bleeding badly, and it seemed ages before an ambulance came.

I remember a man came up, and I said: 'Will you call the police and an ambulance?' He said: 'I am a policeman.' I said: 'Please take this gun and arrest me.'

This statement has been read over to me, and it is true.

(*signed*) RUTH ELLIS

(*No cross-examination.*)

MR STEVENSON, *opening the case for the Defence, told the jury:*

It cannot happen often in this court that in a case of this importance, fraught with such deep significance for the accused, the whole of the prosecution's story passes without any challenge from those concerned to advance the defence.

Let me make this abundantly plain: there is no question here but that this woman shot this man. No one is going to raise any sort of doubt in your mind about that. You will not hear one word from me—or from the lady herself—questioning that.

She is charged with murder, and one of the ingredients in that offence is what lawyers call malice; and the law of England, in its mercy, provides that if a person finding themselves in the position in which this unhappy young woman now is, has been the subject of such emotional disturbance operating upon her mind so as for the time being to unseat her judgment, to inhibit and cut off those censors which ordinarily control our conduct, then it is open to you, the jury who are charged with the dreadful duty of trying her, to say that the offence of which she is guilty is not the offence of murder, but the offence of manslaughter; and that, members of the jury, is what we, on her behalf, ask you to do in this case.

You have nothing to do with morals. The question you have to decide, yea or nay, is whether or not this woman is guilty of brutal murder.

You will hear the sad story of her association with this young man who is now dead. It is always an unpleasant thing to say anything disagreeable about someone who is dead, but I venture to think the story she will unfold to you can leave no doubt in your minds that he was a most unpleasant person.

The fact stands out like a beacon that this young man became an absolute necessity to this young woman. However brutally he behaved, and however much he spent of her money on various entertainments of his own, and however much he consorted with other people, he ultimately came back to her, and always she forgave him. She found herself in something like an emotional prison guarded by this young man, from which there seemed to be no escape.

There is not in this any question of any 'unwritten law', as it is called in some other countries. But when you have heard her in the witness box, you may take the view that there is really no doubt that this young woman was driven by the suffering she endured at the hands of this man to do what she did, and it so operated on her mind that her judgment for the time being was unseated and her understanding was gone, and that malice, which is an essential ingredient in the offence of murder, was absent from this case, so that you can perfectly properly return a verdict of manslaughter rather than a verdict of wilful murder.

Members of the jury, that will depend upon the view you take of this girl when you see her here in the witness box. You will observe that she is now a calm and undisturbed person. You have got to try to put yourselves in the situation in which she found herself during that Easter weekend, when this man, whom she needed as one of the fundamental requirements of her existence, having, as you will hear, promised to spend that weekend with her, having, as you will hear, shortly before amended his conduct and behaved towards her in a way that gave her every hope for the future and bestowed on her all the marks of attention as before, went away and chose to consort with these rather odd people in Hampstead, in whose flat he spent the whole weekend. It was in those circumstances, and driven to a frenzy which for the time being unseated her understanding, that she committed the crime about which you have heard this morning.

You will hear—and I am going to call a very eminent psychologist who will tell you—that the effect of jealousy upon that feminine mind can so work as to unseat the reason and can operate to a degree in which a male mind is quite incapable of operating.

Now, members of the jury, there are dozens and dozens of cases in which the courts have considered this matter which is called provocation. It always has to be considered on the facts which arise in the individual case; but never before, as far as I know, and as far as all the industry of those associated with me can reveal, has any court had to consider a case in which the defence rely upon jealousy, and the state of mind in which a woman gets when a man to whom she is devoted behaves as this one did, as constituting this defence of provocation.

EVIDENCE FOR THE DEFENCE

MRS RUTH ELLIS, *examined by* MR STEVENSON: My marriage has been dissolved; I have two children, a boy of ten and a girl of three and a half. I first met David Blakely in the middle of 1953, when I was working at Carroll's Club. Shortly afterwards, I became manageress of the Little Club, Knightsbridge, and met him again; that was in August 1953. From that time onward, a friendship developed between me and him.

Did he come and live with you in a flat which you occupied above the club?—Yes.

At that time, how did he behave towards you?—He was very concerned about me. He seemed very devoted.

At that time, you were still married?—Yes.

And was he engaged to another young woman?—Yes.

Did he come to sleep at your flat nearly every night, and did he spend the weekends at Penn?—He stayed there from Monday to Friday, and spent the weekends in Penn.

And at that time were you very much in love with him?—Not really.

As time went on, how did he show his feelings for you?—In the December of that year I had an abortion by him, and he was very concerned about my welfare. Although he was engaged to another girl, he offered to marry me, and he said it seemed unnecessary for me to get rid of the child, but I did not want to take advantage of him.

When he offered to marry you, what did you say to that? How did you take it?—I was not really in love with him at the time, and it was quite unnecessary to marry me. I thought I could get out of the mess quite easily.

What mess?—I decided I could get out of the mess quite easily.

MR JUSTICE HAVERS: You mean the child?—Yes.

Without him marrying you?—Yes.

MR STEVENSON: Did you in fact get out of the trouble in the way you have described in February 1954?—That is quite correct.

MR JUSTICE HAVERS: You had an abortion?—Yes.

MR STEVENSON: You knew that Blakely was engaged to be married?—Yes. I didn't take our affair seriously until he had broken it off. I tried to tell him that our association was not good for the club business, and we should stop living together. Mr Blakely didn't like the idea of ending our affair at all.

And so the association continued until the summer of last year?—Yes. David then went away to the Le Mans motor-race, and he stayed away longer than he should have done. That was when my affair with Mr Cussen began.

When you had that affair with Cussen, what did you hope or think might happen as far as Blakely and you were concerned?—I thought it might finish it. I thought that Desmond would tell David we had been intimate, and I thought that would finish it.

But what actually happened?—As soon as Blakely got back, he came straight to see me at the club. I didn't tell him of my affair with Desmond.

But what happened as far as you and Blakely were concerned? —At that time he was getting—David was getting—rather jealous. He asked me what I had been doing, and all kinds of things like that, and, of course, I did not tell him.

Did your association with Blakely in fact end there?—It began again.

At whose insistence? His or yours?—David's.

Did you try to avoid that happening?—It was very difficult. I was running a business, and he was there all the time. He was entitled to walk in. He was a customer, and he was hanging around the bar all the time. He was spending money in my bar. I could not tell him to go away.

Do you remember one night when you were at the flat with him, the question of marriage cropping up between you?—Yes. He asked me to marry him.

MR JUSTICE HAVERS: About when was that?—(*No answer.*)

MR STEVENSON: About how soon after he returned from Le Mans?—I cannot remember the exact date.

Not the exact date. How many days or weeks?—Maybe a couple of weeks. It may have been more. I cannot really remember.

In what terms did he propose to you?—He told me that he would never have any happiness if we didn't get married. He told me that he had broken his engagement off.

What happened to your feelings for him from that time onwards?—He was a very likeable person, and I got very attached to him.

Did you think you could trust him?—He had given me reason not to trust him. One night he got into bed and was stretching over to switch out the light when I noticed love bites all over his shoulders, back and neck. I went quite cold with shock, and I told him to get out and leave the flat. He said he could explain everything and started to tell me that someone had bitten him in the neck while he was playing darts at Penn. I said: 'Please get out of my bed and out of my flat, and don't come near me again.'

Was there a row about it?—No, I just asked him to go. He did not like it, but he went.

How long did he remain away?—He 'phoned about an hour after he had left the premises, and he 'phoned early in the morning and told me he had spent the night at Islington, and he was very cold and miserable and asked if he could come back, and I said: 'No.' He returned as soon as the bar opened up at three o'clock, and went into my bar, and asked my barmaid if he could see me, and I had already instructed the barmaid that I was not at home to him. He 'phoned then from the box just in the entrance to the club to my place upstairs, and asked if he could please come up, and I said: 'No.' After half an hour he came upstairs, and I was fooling around in the flat, doing one thing and another. He was very emotionally upset, and he went on his knees, crying and saying: 'I'm sorry, darling. I do love you. I'll prove it,' and he asked me to marry him, and I said: 'I don't think your mother or family will agree to this.'

What did he say about that?—He said that if there was any trouble with his family, we could get married secretly.

Is it right to say that, at this time, the proceedings for the dissolution of your marriage were going on?—Yes.

How did they terminate? First of all, was it a defended divorce case?—No, I did not defend myself.

Not in the end, but had it been defended up to that time?—Yes, yes.

Why did it cease to be defended?—Because I wanted a divorce, and I decided not to claim any maintenance or defend myself in any way and also to give up my daughter.

Did the divorce go through?—Yes, undefended.

You say you did that on the ground that you were going to marry David, is that right?—Yes.

Blakely continued to live with you at the Little Club?—Yes.

Where you paid rent for the flat?—Yes.

How much?—£10 a week.

What was his financial situation?—He appeared to have money until his engagement was broken, but then he said he was broke.

Did you help him?—I gave him money, bought him clothes, and paid for his cigarettes and drink bill.

Did he explain why he was short of money?—I knew racing cars were very expensive. He was paying Mr Findlater £10 a week to work on his car, and, naturally, all his money was going on racing cars. He was not earning anything. He used to stay at his mother's flat at Penn, and he came into the club one night to say he had had a row with his step-father, who had threatened to cut off his allowance. He said he was going to commit suicide.

Did he pay for drinks at the club?—I had given the barmaid instructions that if he came to the bar he was to be allowed to drink without paying. He used to eat at the club, and when we went out I gave him the money. If he made out a cheque, I gave him the money afterwards to meet it.

By October 1954, was there a further change in his behaviour towards you? How did he treat you physically?—He was violent on occasions.

What sort of violence?—It was always because of jealousy in the bar. At the end of the evening when we got upstairs, it was always about the things he had been seeing me do, and so on and so forth.

How did this violence manifest itself?—He only used to hit me with his fists and his hands, but I bruise very easily, and I was full of bruises on many occasions.

When he complained about your working in the club, and exhibiting this jealousy, how did you take it?—I often told him to please go and not come back, sort of thing, but whether I meant it or not, I said it anyway.

When you said that, did he ever go?—No.

(*Luncheon adjournment.*)

Answering further questions from MR STEVENSON, *the defendant testified:* Towards the end of last year, I decided to leave the club; I thought it was one way of breaking up the affair with Blakely. I took a course in modelling and also took French lessons to prepare to earn a living away from the club. I left the club in December.

MR STEVENSON: And where did you go?—I moved to Mr Desmond Cussen's flat, Goodwood Court, Devonshire Street.

And what was Blakely's attitude to your doing that?—He did not like me going to live with Desmond at the flat. Last Christmas Night, he arrived at the flat and there was a scene.

Did you often see him at Goodwood Court?—When Mr Cussen was away, David and I used the flat.

In February of this year, was there another scene?—Yes. We had been drinking quite a lot.

And did you sustain injuries?—I sprained my ankle, got lots of bruises and a black eye. But I think David realised he had gone too far, for I was really hurt.

The next day, did Mr Cussen take you to Middlesex Hospital to have the injuries treated?—Yes.

After this scene, Blakely sent you carnations?—Yes.

Was this card enclosed?—(*Exhibit produced to the witness.*) Yes.

Please read it.—'Sorry, darling. I love you. David.'

After this, you made up your quarrel?—Yes. I took the flat in Egerton Gardens, and David came to live with me.

I do not want to mention names, but after you had been there a short while, was there some trouble about a young woman?—Yes.

And, again without mentioning names, was that woman down at Penn, or Beaconsfield?—In Penn.

And did you on one occasion remain all night outside the house where that other woman was living?—Yes.

And did you see Blakely come out in the morning?—He came

out at nine o'clock in the morning. He had hidden his car at the back of the Crown public house, which is just down the road.

What were your feelings at that time?—I was obviously jealous of him now. I mean the tables had been turned. I was jealous of him whereas he, before, had been jealous of me. I had now given up my business—what he had wanted me to do—left all my friends behind connected with clubs and things, and it was my turn to be jealous of him.

How did you react?—I told him we were finished and it was all done with. I asked him for the key of the flat back, but he would not give it to me. He returned to the flat after an absence of about a week.

Why did you take him back?—For the same reason: because I was in love with him.

Were you anxious to take him back?—Oh, yes.

In March, did you find that you were pregnant?—Yes.

At the end of March, did you do anything about that pregnancy? What happened about it?—Well, we had a fight a few days previously—I forget the exact time—and David got very, very violent. I do not know whether that caused the miscarriage or not, but he did thump me in the tummy.

And that was followed by a miscarriage?—Yes.

When Blakely first knew that you were pregnant, how did he behave?—He seemed to want me to have the child. But later his attitude changed, and he said things like: 'Well, I can just about afford seven shillings a week.'

At the beginning of April you went with Blakely to the motor racing at Oulton Park?—Yes.

What happened at that time?—His car broke down in practice, and he blamed me for this because I had told him previously that he would have no luck because of the way he was treating me. When we got back to London, I was ill in bed with a cold, and for the first two evenings back he arrived home very late. I discovered that he was at the Steering Wheel with friends.

How did you feel about that?—I felt nothing but contempt for him.

The following night—this was the Wednesday before Easter—did he come home early?—Yes.

Was there any change in his mood or behaviour towards you?—

Well, he seemed entirely different again. He was quite happy, and he was saying everything would be all right, we would soon have some money, and talking about marriage again and all kinds of other little things.

Did he bring anything on that occasion?—Yes, he brought me the latest photograph he had had taken.

Was that a recent photograph?—It was a photograph he had had taken. He was going to race a car, a Bristol, at Le Mans this year, and he had to have a photograph taken, you see, and he had an enlargement which I had.

He brought it to you, did he?—Yes.

Did he write on it in your presence?—Yes. 'To Ruth with all my love, from David.'

Is that the photograph?—(*Exhibit produced to the witness.*) Yes. (*The witness began to cry.*)

MR STEVENSON: My Lord, I wonder if she could sit down?

MR JUSTICE HAVERS: Yes, certainly.

THE WITNESS: No, it is quite all right.

MR JUSTICE HAVERS: Do, by all means.

THE WITNESS: I do not want to sit down.

MR STEVENSON: Did he stay in that evening and that night? How were you, the two of you?—We were very happy.

Was there some discussion about how you could raise some money?—David said he was going to sell his racing car. I did not want him to.

Why not?—Because he was so fond of motor racing. It seemed such a shame. He had built a car and then wanted to sell it. He said: 'If you can find me £400, I won't need to sell it.'

On Thursday, the 7th, had you booked seats for the theatre?—Yes.

And he arrived in time for the theatre?—No. He 'phoned to say he was in a traffic jam, which was quite correct because he must have been 'phoning from a 'phone box somewhere on Western Avenue. I could hear cars and things. He was obviously stuck in a traffic jam.

And did you, in fact, go to a film instead?—Yes.

How were you getting on?—All through the cinema, which was rather annoying, he was telling me he loved me and all kinds of things—and a very good film. He seemed very attentive to me.

And did you make—or did you discuss any plans on that occasion as to what you were going to do the following Easter weekend?—Yes. I understood we were going motor racing on the Monday.

How were you going to spend the remainder of the Easter weekend?—We were going to take Andria out—we were going to take my son out. Mr Blakely was very fond of my son.

Now, on the morning of Good Friday, the 8th, did he leave?—Yes.

What did he say he was going to do?—He left me about ten o'clock in the morning and said he was going to meet Anthony.

Anthony Findlater?—Yes.

On what sort of terms did you part on Good Friday morning?—On the very best of terms. He arranged to come back at eight o'clock to collect me for a drink with the Findlaters.

Did he return that evening?—No. I got back to the flat at half-past seven to wait for him, but he did not turn up. After waiting till about 9.30, I telephoned the Findlaters.

Who answered the telephone?—Anthony Findlater.

What did you say to him?—I said to him: 'Anthony, is David with you?'

Yes?—And he said: 'No.' So I said: 'I am very worried because he should have been back to meet me.' I said: 'Do you think he is all right?' Mr Findlater replied and said: 'Oh, he is all right.'

Did he tell you where he was?—Yes. Just before that he said that he had seen him earlier but that he had left.

When you were told that he had left, did you believe it?—Not the way he said it. He said it rather cocky, as though, you know . . . well, I do not know quite how to say it.

What was your reaction?—I was furious because I was expecting David to come back, and I was not feeling very well. We had planned to spend the weekend together.

What did you do?—I rang Mr Cussen and said I wanted to go to Hampstead. He asked me what I wanted there, and I said I just wanted to see if David's Vanguard car was at the flat at Hampstead. He drove me there, and I saw the car outside. I was furious, and rang the door-bell, but they would not answer it, though I rang and rang. When I telephoned from a call box, they put the receiver down. I was absolutely furious with David. I just wanted to see him and ask for the keys back—all kinds of things were going on. I just wanted him to jump in the lake, or go and lose himself—something silly. I went back to the house and rang the door-bell again. I heard female giggles coming from the flat.

What did you do next?—Well, my intention was to make a noise to make them come and open the front door. I was feeling just a little—in a peculiar mood then: rather a nasty mood to make them open the door, that was all.

What did you in fact do?—Well, I knew the Vanguard windows were only stuck in with rubber, so I pushed at one of them and it came clean out from the rubber. It did not break it, just made a noise. And I did the same with two other windows. I did not break any, I just pushed them in. The next thing I knew was the arrival of the police. I was advised to go home.

Did you take this advice?—Eventually, yes.

What sort of night did you have?—I did not go to sleep. I just smoked. I was still in a temper. I was very upset about the whole thing, to think that David was behaving so disgustingly now. I was not well.

We now come to the events of Easter Saturday. Did you go back to Tanza Road?—Yes. I watched the flat at intervals throughout the day.

Why did you do that?—Like a typically jealous woman, I thought there was something going on which I should know about. In the afternoon, I stood in a doorway two houses away from the Findlaters' flat, and was invited into the house to tea. I stayed an hour, and was able to watch everything that was going on. I saw the Findlaters and David drive up.

Did you then leave?—Yes. I returned in the evening.

What did you see?—Obviously a party was taking place then.

MR JUSTICE HAVERS: Where were you this time?—Oh, just up the road. Just standing in the road.

There was obviously a party going on in Mr Findlater's flat, is that what you say?—Yes. The window was open, and there seemed to be a lot of noise coming from there.

MR STEVENSON: And voices you were able to hear?—Yes.

Did you recognise any voice?—Yes, I heard David's voice.

Any female voice?—Yes, I heard somebody giggling a lot. I had an idea it was somebody I knew, but—

While you were watching there that evening, did you see any people come up to the house?—Yes, an open sports car pulled up, and a man and a woman got out.

Who were they?—I think it was Clive, but I would not be quite sure that it was.

Clive would be Gunnell?—Yes.

And with him a woman?—Yes.

And how late did you remain watching that night?—It must have been about half-past nine or—half-past nine to ten, if not earlier—when David and Anthony came down the steps with a woman. I was standing by the side of Anthony's house.

MR JUSTICE HAVERS: David and?—David and a woman and Mr Findlater came down the steps of Mr Findlater's flat.

MR STEVENSON: Yes?—I was standing at the side of the flat. I heard David say—

MR JUSTICE HAVERS: Wait a minute. Yes?—I heard David say: 'Let me put my arm round you for support.' If they had turned round, they would have seen me.

Yes?

MR STEVENSON: Could you see who he was addressing when he said that?—I presumed it was the nanny, but I had never seen her before, except for a glimpse in the afternoon.

How old was she, roughly?—Young, I should think. She was dark, I know that.

How long did you remain there that night?—Quite late. Twelve o'clock.

What?—About 12.30.

MR JUSTICE HAVERS: I do not quite know what happened. Did they go off in the car?—They went off in the car, yes.

MR STEVENSON: You remained there until 12.30. Did you see them come back?—I went away and came back again.

At what time did you come back?—When I came back, the cars were back again, so I gathered they had arrived back.

You remained there until after midnight. Was the party still going on?—Yes.

Again, were you able to distinguish any voices?—Yes, the window was open.

Whose voices could you hear?—I heard Anthony's, and I heard David's, and I heard a woman giggling again.

Did you know from earlier visits to the flat where the nanny slept?—Yes. Mrs Findlater had told me a couple of weeks before that the landlord of the flats, or the house, was going to let her have one of his rooms, his front room, which they were doing up for the nanny.

Was that above or below the Findlaters' flat?—Below—with a separate front door.

As you were there, did you see anything happen?—Between ten o'clock and 10.30 the nanny had obviously gone to her room, but the blinds were not down, and her light was on, and the light in the passage was on.

And then?—The party still continued, and the car that had driven up, the old sports car, was still outside, and I still heard the woman giggling. About 12.30, the blind in the nanny's room went down, and the light in the hall went out.

MR JUSTICE HAVERS: The blind in the nanny's room went down, and the light in the hall—what?—Went out as well, and that was at 12.30.

MR STEVENSON: Were you able to hear Blakely's voice all the time?—After that, no. I could not hear it, although I listened for it.

After when?—After 12.30 I could not hear it.

MR JUSTICE HAVERS: The lights were out everywhere?—No. The blind in the nanny's room had gone down, and the light in the hall turned out.

Was there a light anywhere else?—Yes, the party was still going on.

MR STEVENSON: The nanny had gone to bed and pulled down the blind, and at that time you no longer heard David's voice?—That is right. He could have been still there, but I did not hear his voice.

The party was still going on, is that correct?—Yes.

Rightly or wrongly, what did you think was happening?—I thought David was up to his tricks he was always doing.

What sort of tricks?—Knowing David, I thought he might be having an affair with somebody else.

With whom?—Perhaps the nanny might be the new attraction.

Ultimately, did you go home?—Yes.

And again, what sort of night did you have?—I did not sleep again.

And what state of mind were you in?—I was very, very upset.

The next morning, which was the Easter Sunday, did you telephone the flat again?—Yes. I thought if David was sleeping in the lounge, and the divan is next to the 'phone, he would be the first to pick it up.

Was it in the lounge he used to sleep when he went there?—Yes. There is no other room—only one bedroom and a small room.

You telephoned?—Yes, just before nine.

What happened?—What I thought would happen: the 'phone would either be answered by David, or picked up immediately and taken off to stop it from ringing. I waited a long time before it was answered, and then Anthony answered the 'phone.

That is Findlater?—Yes.

What did you say?—I think I said: 'I hope you are having an enjoyable holiday, because you have ruined mine.'

Did you remain in your flat until lunchtime?—Just before lunch, yes.

What did you do then?—Mr Cussen picked me up with my son, and we went over, and I took something to eat at Mr Cussen's flat, and we spent some time in the flat.

As far as the morning is concerned, were you waiting for a telephone call?—Yes, I thought David would still 'phone.

And he did not?—No.

How did you spend the afternoon?—I have completely forgotten what I did now. My son was with us, and we amused him in some way. I do not know what I did.

At what time did you put the child to bed?—About 7.30.

Was there still no message from Blakely?—No.

MR JUSTICE HAVERS: You had gone back to your flat by this time, had you?—Yes.

MR STEVENSON: And what did you do next?—I put my son to bed.

Yes. Go on.—I was very upset, and I had a peculiar idea I wanted to kill him.

You had what?—I had an idea I wanted to kill him.

And we have had the evidence about your taking a revolver up to Hampstead and shooting him. Is that right?—Quite correct.

Why did you do it?—I do not really know, quite seriously. I was just very upset.

MR JUSTICE HAVERS: 'I do not really know why I shot him.' Is that right?—Yes.

'I was very upset'?—Yes.

MR STEVENSON: When you say you had a peculiar idea that you wanted to kill him, were you able to control it?—No.

And then you went up, in fact, and shot him. Is that right?—Yes.

Cross-examined by MR HUMPHREYS:

Mrs Ellis, when you fired that revolver at close range into the body of David Blakely, what did you intend to do?—It is obvious that when I shot him I intended to kill him.

Thank you.

DR DUNCAN WHITTAKER, *examined by* MR STEVENSON: I am a Master of Arts, a Member of the Royal College of Surgeons, and a Licentiate of the Royal College of Physicians; I also hold a diploma in psychological medicine. I agree with the view of Professor Jung that women cannot so easily as men separate their sexual experiences with men from their total personal relationships.

You mean that a man's love is a man's boast, a woman's is her existence?—They are more prone to hysterical reactions than men.

And under the influence of these hysterical reactions, what becomes of their standards of conduct and control?—They are inclined to lose some of their inhibitory capacity and solve their problems on a more primitive level. This is not applying to women in general, but if they do have hysterical reactions, they are more prone to hysterical reactions than men. A man in the firing line in a war sometimes gets a paralysis that ensures his removal from the front—

MR JUSTICE HAVERS: I thought we were talking about women. What has the firing line got to do with a woman? If you want to talk about men, very well, but I thought we were talking about this woman.

MR STEVENSON: Did you interview Mrs Ellis at Holloway Prison on 4 June?—Yes.

How long were you with her?—Two hours.

What was your main impression?—The feature which impressed me most was her equanimity. She had drifted into a situation which was for her intolerable, but she could find no way out, and she had not a sufficiently hysterical personality to solve her problems by a complete loss of memory.

Were you able to form any view as to her state of mind on the day she shot this man?—She was very disturbed.

Yes. What else?

MR JUSTICE HAVERS: Are you talking about the day of the shooting, or the day you saw her?—The day of the shooting. She was not disturbed when I saw her. I think her mind was very definitely disturbed on that day.

In what way?—The situation was now absolutely intolerable for her. She considered that he was being unfaithful at that moment, but she was convinced that he would return and she would not be able to resist him.

MR STEVENSON: Were you able to form any view about the subject of jealousy?—Yes. At that time she both hated him and loved him. She had ambivalent emotions.

When you get that duality of emotion, what does that indicate, so far as the patient is concerned?—Some degree of emotional immaturity—not intellectual but emotional.

MR JUSTICE HAVERS: She had some degree of emotional immaturity?—Yes.

MR STEVENSON: Did you ask her any questions with a view to finding out whether she considered the consequences of what she was doing?—I asked her if she thought about her children. She said she did not think about them at all.

Having regard to the fact that she is, as you say, emotionally immature, and also that jealousy has the effect that you have indicated on a woman, and bearing in mind your own examination of Mrs Ellis, what view have you formed about this occurrence on Easter Sunday?—I have formed the view that if Blakely had given her the chance to blow him up on the telephone, the emotional tension would have been released, and the incident would not have occurred.

Cross-examined by MR HUMPHREYS:

Dr Whittaker, do you regard her as being somewhat emotionally immature?—Yes.

From the psychological point of view, something of an hysteric?—Yes, but not a gross hysteric.

In your view, there was such emotional tension over the week-end, without relief, that she was impelled to resort to violent action to release that suppressed emotion?—Yes.

In your view, at the time of the killing, she was mentally capable of forming the intent to kill?—Yes.

In your view, was she at the time, within the meaning of the English law, sane or insane?—Sane.

MR STEVENSON: That is my case, my Lord.

MR JUSTICE HAVERS *released the jury, telling them that there were matters of law to be discussed which need not trouble them.*

MR STEVENSON *submitted that the provocation which the defendant had experienced through jealousy during her association with David Blakely had affected her mind to an extent that would justify a verdict of manslaughter. This provoked an exclamation from* MR JUSTICE HAVERS: 'But this is new law!' MR STEVENSON *admitted that the Defence had been unable to find a precedent either in this country or in the United States of America for a court's considering* 'the effect on the female mind of infidelity in a spouse or a lover'.

MR JUSTICE HAVERS: That is very curious after all these years, because jealousy is one of the commonest emotions . . . Does your proposition come to this, putting it in its simplest form: if a man associates with a woman, and he then leaves her suddenly, and does not communicate with her, and she is a jealous woman, emotionally disturbed, and goes out and shoots him, that is sufficient ground for the jury to reduce the crime of murder to manslaughter?

MR STEVENSON *was unable to give a direct answer to the judge's question.*

MR HUMPHREYS: I accept my learned friend's proposition that this woman was disgracefully treated by the man who died, and I accept my learned friend's proposition that it would tend to lead her into an intensely emotional condition, even as that hypothetical person, 'the ordinary, reasonable human being'. These conditions may well apply elsewhere. But was she brought more than into a state where it would be reasonable for her to hit and hurt him? One must take into account that the actual crime was planned and prepared. There was some pursuit of that purpose through the streets of London, and during the time of an hour or two; and finally, the man she killed was an unarmed man, and without any semblance of a struggle, she shot him in the back.

The court adjourned until 10.30 am the following day.

SECOND DAY

Tuesday, 21 June 1955

In the absence of the jury.

MR JUSTICE HAVERS: I feel constrained to rule that there is not sufficient material, even on a view of the evidence most favourable to the accused, for a reasonable jury to form the view that a reasonable person so provoked could be driven, through transport of passion and loss of self-control, to the degree and method and continuance of violence which produced the death, and consequently it is my duty as a judge, and as a matter of law, to direct the jury that the evidence in this case does not support a verdict of manslaughter on the grounds of provocation.

MR STEVENSON: In view of the ruling which your Lordship has just pronounced, it is desirable that I should say that I cannot now with propriety address the jury at all, because it would be impossible for me to do so without inviting the jury to disregard your Lordship's ruling.

The jury returned to court.

MR STEVENSON *explained to the jury that there would be no closing speech for the Defence.*

MR HUMPHREYS: In the circumstances, I have nothing to say.

THE SUMMING-UP

MR JUSTICE HAVERS *told the jury:*

You will approach this case without any thoughts of sympathy either for the man or for the accused, who is a young woman—and, you may think, a young woman badly treated by the deceased man. Nothing of that sort must enter into your consideration. You will arrive at your verdict fearlessly, without any thought of the consequences one way or the other. You will arrive at your verdict solely on the evidence you have heard in this court.

Mrs Ellis is charged with wilful murder, which in our law is the unlawful killing of one person by another with malice. What is meant by malice is this: the formation of an intention either to kill or to do grievous bodily harm. Long premeditation is unnecessary; the intention either to kill or to do grievous bodily harm can be formed at any moment of time up to the moment when the act is done. But there must be intent, and in considering such a matter you should have regard to the type of weapon used: whether it is a lethal weapon or not.

In this case, six shots were fired by a Smith & Wesson revolver—a lethal weapon. Three or four were fired into the body of Blakely, and one was fired at extremely close range. In order to fire the revolver, there had to be pressure on the trigger each time. Having regard to the nature of the weapon, the number of shots fired, and the fact that the gun has to be cocked each time, you will have to ask yourselves this very serious question: whether you would not be compelled to the conclusion that there was, in the circumstances of this case, at least an intention to do grievous bodily harm, if not to kill.

If all the evidence compels you to that conclusion, and you are satisfied that Mrs Ellis intentionally fired the shots, then that would amount to a verdict of guilty of murder.

You may think it very difficult for a person who fires a revolver of that type six times and hits a person three or four times with shots from it to have any other than an intention to do at least bodily harm.

If a person does an act towards another wilfully which a reasonable person would know can cause death or grievous bodily harm, and death results, that is murder. If the person could not have contemplated either of those circumstances, she would be guilty only of manslaughter, which is the unlawful killing of one person by another without malice—that is to say, without the intention to kill or to do grievous bodily harm.

You should have regard to the statements Mrs Ellis made after her arrest, and to those which she has given in evidence.

At first, she made a statement saying that she was guilty, but apparently that was before she was charged with any offence. She then went on to explain how she got the revolver, and later how she took the gun and shot Blakely. She said in her statement: 'I thought I had missed him, so I fired again.'

In the witness box, she said she was very upset and wanted to kill Blakely. She said: 'I do not know why I shot him—I was just very upset.' Replying to Mr Humphreys's one question in cross-examination, her answer was: 'When I fired the revolver at close range, I intended to kill him.'

Members of the jury, that is the crucial issue for you to decide in this case. Are you satisfied—and it is not challenged by the Defence—that she fired those shots deliberately into the body of Blakely?

After reviewing the prosecution evidence of the happenings on the night of 10 April, MR JUSTICE HAVERS *repeated his ruling, given in the absence of the jury, that the evidence did not support a verdict of manslaughter on the grounds of provocation. He added:*

It is not a defence to prove that she was a jealous woman, and you may think her evidence strengthens the case for the prosecution, because she said: 'I wanted to kill David.'

I am bound to tell you that even if you accept the full evidence of this woman, it does not seem to me that it establishes any sort of defence to the charge of murder. According to our law, members of the jury, it is no defence for a woman who is charged with the murder of her lover to prove that she was a jealous woman and had been badly treated by her lover and was in ill-health, and that, after her lover promised to spend the Easter holidays with her, he left her without any warning and refused to communicate with her, or that he spent holidays with his friend, or in the company of another woman, or that he was committing misconduct with another woman, and that, as a result of that, she became furious with him and emotionally upset and formed an intention to kill him which she could not control. None of these facts individually affords any defence, nor do they collectively afford any defence.

There is one other observation which I should like to make, and that is that this court is not a court of morals. You will not, therefore, allow your judgment to be swayed or your minds prejudiced in the least degree because, on her own admission, when Mrs Ellis was a married woman she committed adultery, or because she was having two persons at different times as lovers. Dismiss those questions from your minds.

There is no evidence whatever that Mrs Ellis was, at the time when she did this act, insane. The Defence did not seek to put that forward, and it is a matter which is not open to you to consider in this case.

If you are satisfied that the accused deliberately fired those shots at Blakely, and as a result he died, it is not open to you to find a verdict of not guilty.

If, on a review of the whole evidence, you are left in reasonable doubt whether at the time she fired those shots she intended to kill or do grievous bodily harm, you will find her guilty of manslaughter.

If, on the consideration of the whole evidence, you are satisfied that at the time she fired those shots she had the intention of killing or doing grievous bodily harm, then your duty is to find her guilty of wilful murder.

The jury retired at 11.52 am and returned at 12.15 pm.

VERDICT AND SENTENCE

THE CLERK OF THE COURT: Members of the jury, will your foreman please stand? Mr Foreman of the jury, are you agreed upon your verdict?

THE FOREMAN: We are.

THE CLERK: Do you find the prisoner at the Bar, Ruth Ellis, guilty or not guilty of the murder of David Blakely?

THE FOREMAN: Guilty.

THE CLERK: You find her guilty, and that is the verdict of you all?

THE FOREMAN: Yes.

THE CLERK: Prisoner at the Bar, you stand convicted of murder. Have you anything to say before judgment of death is passed according to law?

THE PRISONER: *No reply.*

MR JUSTICE HAVERS: Ruth Ellis, the jury have convicted you of murder. In my view, it was the only verdict possible. The sentence of the Court upon you is that you be taken hence to a lawful prison, and thence to a place of execution, and that you there be hanged by the neck until you be dead, and that your body be buried within the precincts of the prison within which you shall last have been confined before your execution, and may the Lord have mercy upon your soul.

THE CHAPLAIN: Amen.

POST-MORTEM EXAMINATION.

Name	ELLIS, Ruth	**Apparent Age**	28 years
At	H.M. Prison, Holloway	**Date**	July 13 1955

EXTERNAL EXAMINATION	
Nourishment	Well nourished. Evidence of proper care and attention. Height - 5ft. 2ins. Weight - 103 lbs.
Marks of Violence, Identification, etc. ...	DEEP IMPRESSIONS AROUND NECK of noose with suspension point about 1 inch in front of the angle of the L.lower jaw. Vital changes locally and in the tissues beneath as a consequence of sudden constriction. No ecchymoses in the face - or, indeed, elsewhere. No marks of restraint.
How long dead	1 hour.
INTERNAL EXAMINATION	
Skull	Fracture-dislocation of the spine at C.2 with a 2 inch gap and transverse separation of the spinal cord at the same level.
Brain Meninges	
Mouth, Tongue, Oesophagus	Fractures of both wings of the hyoid and the R.wing of the thyroid cartilage. Larynx also fractured.
Larynx, Trachea, Lungs ...	Air passages clear and lungs quite free from disease or other change. No engorgement. No asphyxial changes.
Pericardium, Heart and Blood Vessels	No organic disease. No petechiae or other evidence of asphyxial change.
Stomach and Contents ...	Small food residue, and odour of brandy. No disease.
Peritoneum, Intestines, Etc.	Normal.
Liver and Gall Bladder ...	Terminal congestion only.
Spleen	Normal.
Kidneys and Ureters... ...	Slight terminal congestion only.
Bladder, Etc.	
Generative Organs	Lower abdominal operation scar for ectopic pregnancy operation in L.tube, now healed. No pregnancy.
Other Remarks	Deceased was a healthy subject at the time of death. Mark of suspension normally situated and injuries from judicial hanging - to the spinal columnand cord - such as must have caused instant death.
CAUSE OF DEATH ...	Injuries to the central nervous system consequent upon judicial hanging.

Signed Keith Simpson

M.D. Lond.
146, Harley St., W.1, and Guy's Hospital (Pathologist)
Reader in Forensic Medicine, London University.

APPENDIX 1

Article by 'Cassandra' (William Connor) in the *Daily Mirror*, 30 June 1955

Should Ruth Ellis Hang?

On July 13 Ruth Ellis is due to be taken to a place of execution and there to suffer death by hanging and her body buried in the precincts of the prison where she has been confined.

The jury in this case swiftly pronounced her guilty within twenty-three minutes.

They made no recommendation to mercy.

The judge said that no other verdict was possible.

Her lawyers decided to make no appeal.

Death at the hands of the public hangman is very near and only the Home Secretary, left with the last agonising decision, can save her from a shameful doom in a prison yard.

It is unlikely that he will do so.

What sort of a killing was this?

It was a fierce, white-hot murder. Ruth Ellis fired six shots at her lover. Four of them hit him. She had to pull back the trigger for every shot she aimed at him.

It was not one continuous burst of fire but six separate, deliberate operations. One deadly wound resulted from the muzzle of the gun being held within three inches of the dying man's body.

Pity comes hard after such dreadful deeds. Compassion weeps but is silent.

Yet had I the power I would save her. This was a murder of love and hate. The one as fierce as the other—the storm of tenderness matching the fury of revenge.

In human nature, where passion is involved, love and hate walk hand in hand and side by side.

The difference between them is a hair's-breadth. The one can change to the other in a trice. Infinite sweetness and affection become infinite wickedness and black insensate cruelty.

This was no slow poisoning. But a sudden explosion of the forces of evil that are latent in the hearts of more men and women than would care to admit it—terrible, senseless, evil, and all too human.

There are thirteen more days to go.

By the nature of her crime, by the nature of her appearance, by the ingrained horror that most people have at the prospect of a woman shortly to be dragged to the scaffold, it is inevitable that millions of people will be increasingly drawn towards the shortening shadow of the hideous event to come.

Some will be fascinated—morbidly so. Others will be horrified and haunted.

But there will be an almost tribal unanimity in the interest of the case. It is part of the degrading price that capital punishment demands—and always gets.

Justice not only has to be done, but it also has to be seen to be done. And so have the barbaric penalties of execution. They, too, have to be seen to be done.

This ghastly business, this obscene ritual which we, who claim to be the most civilised people in the world, have never succeeded in getting rid of, is witnessed by many people—most of whom have the decency to want to vomit.

The sheriff has to be there. The gaoler, the surgeon, the chaplain and the hangman are present, 'and such other persons as the sheriff requires or allows'.

These by law may even include the relatives of the prisoner, and any Justice of the Peace for the county who wants a ghastly day out.

You who read this paper—and millions like you—are the key supporters of this sickening system whereby with panoply and brutality mixed with the very dubious sauce of religion and consolation we bury our worst malefactors in the quicklime grave.

You may shy away from your terrible responsibility and say that justice has been done.

But justice is not full retribution. Justice is not maximum vengeance, and if it were, the bursting gaols that we now have would be ten times more overcrowded and the gibbets would creak in every county in the land.

The prospect of judicial execution never stopped any murderer.

By all the records that have ever been examined, the scaffold does not prevent the use of the gun, the knife, the fatal blow, the strangler's hands or the phial of poison.

Ruth Ellis does not matter any more than her two most recent female predecessors to the hangman's noose—Mrs Merrifield and Mrs Christophi.

But what we do to her—you and I—matters very much. And if we do it, and if we continue to do it to her sad successors, then we all bear the guilt of savagery untinged with mercy.

APPENDIX 2

Letters published in the London *Evening Standard*, 30 June–12 July 1955

30 June
As a part-time resident and full-time friend and admirer of England, I have always, until now, respected its legal system—as has most of the world. But there is at times a vein of savagery that repels me.

I have been tormented for a week at the idea that a highly civilised people should put a rope around the neck of Ruth Ellis and drop her through a trap and break her neck. I could understand perhaps the hanging of a woman for bestial crime like a multiple poisoning, an axe murder (à la Lizzie Borden) or a baby-farm operator killing her charges, but this was a crime of passion under considerable provocation. No other country in the world would hang this woman.

In France she would get off with a light sentence or none. In America it would be first or second degree manslaughter and she would be out of prison in anywhere from three and a half to seven years.

This thing haunts and, so far as I may say it, disgusts me as something obscene. I am not referring to the trial, of course, but to the medieval savagery of the law.

Raymond Chandler,
Eaton Square, Westminster

1 July
Raymond Chandler criticises the English legal system for its 'savagery' if the death sentence on Mrs Ruth Ellis is carried out.

This woman was convicted of the *wilful* murder of David Blakely and, in view of the well-known circumstances of the crime, no substantial defence was, or could have been, put forward on her behalf.

For such a crime English law exacts the extreme penalty, and the facts that the perpetrator was a woman and her suggested motive jealousy cannot in the interests of justice be allowed to mitigate the punishment.

It is true that in France and America you can kill and get away with, at most, two or three years in jail. In France they call it 'Crime Passionel,' whatever that may mean, and in America they have no name for it but you get away with it in the same way.

In this country, if you murder you pay the penalty. If there are any extenuating circumstances then the Home Secretary may advise Her Majesty to exercise her prerogative of mercy. But the fact remains that the person has 'killed.' In this country you may not kill with impunity, thank God.

Arnold K. Maplesden,
Canonbury Square, Islington

I was delighted to read Mr Raymond Chandler's protest against the proposed hanging of Ruth Ellis. He says he has been 'tormented' by the thought of this horror. Quite so: it always amazes me that so many people can read of an impending execution, and then dismiss the matter from their minds.

There will, no doubt, be the usual hack retorts: 'Have you no pity for the man she killed?' Of course I have; but you don't put one murder right by committing another one.

I am reminded of words written by Thackeray after witnessing an execution: 'I came away from Snow Hill that morning with a disgust for murder, but it was for the murder I saw done. I pray to Almighty God to cause this disgraceful sin to pass from among us, and to cleanse our land of blood.'

Victor Gollancz,
Henrietta Street, Westminster

It is a terrible comment on our laws that a writer of American murder stories should be the first to protest against the imminent hanging of Ruth Ellis.

The only justification for the retention of capital punishment is that it is said to be a deterrent. But a deterrent for whom? Well, if Ruth Ellis is hanged, clearly she will be deterred from repeating her crime; yet so equally would she by a term of imprisonment.

Murder is not a habitual crime: there are plenty of reprieved murderers in our midst and they have not, as far as I know, been apprehended a second time.

As for the argument that her execution will deter others, it is not generally realised that the great majority of murders are wholly unpremeditated.

Capital punishment has been abolished in Austria, Belgium, Denmark, Finland, Holland, Norway, Portugal, Sweden, Switzerland.

There is no evidence in any of these countries that abolition was followed by an increase in murder.

Are we English so very different?

Ludovic Kennedy,
Church Row, Hampstead

2 July

Mr Raymond Chandler's excellent letter echoes the views of many people. In a country that claims to lead the world in matters of reform, capital punishment is, indeed, a blot.

If one could, truly, believe that the death penalty is a deterrent to the would-be murderer, possibly one should suppress one's revulsion against it—but this has never been proved to be so. Those who say that they would never commit a murder for fear of being hanged are those who would never commit a murder under any circumstances.

Surely it is time that we followed the example of the 30 other states who have abolished capital punishment with no evidence of any increase in the murder rate, and did away with the gallows.

Joan Henry,
Beaufort Gardens, Chelsea

I agree with Mr Raymond Chandler that in no country that we recognise as civilised, other than Britain, would this unfortunate girl be put to death. In America, as in France, there is public acquiescence in the death penalty for crimes of brutality, for the husband who insures his wife's life and then poisons her, and the rapist who murders his victim to cover his crime.

But, in cases where the murder was one of impulse or where there was an emotional fixation, the public refuse to sanction an execution, seeing the difference between this class of murder and those I mention above.

In America, where I live for half the year, people still talk of the hypocrisy of the English in having hanged Edith Thompson without compunction because she was an immoral woman. I am sure we will be similarly arraigned in the years to come if we take the life of this young woman.

Let us hope the Home Secretary of today is not as deaf to modern expressions of opinion as was his predecessor of 30 years ago.

Guy Bolton,
Devonshire Court, Marylebone

It may sound harsh, but I think that Ruth Ellis should hang. She was convicted of a cold-blooded murder, and we do not recognise crimes passionelle in this country.

In the same way as Derek Bentley was hanged for his part in the shooting of a policeman at Croydon, justice must be maintained.

Dennis Wheatley,
Grove Place, Great Lymington, Hants.

I have read your reports on Ruth Ellis, and I am of the opinion that she must pay the price for murder.

I was at her trial at the Old Bailey and sat just behind Ruth Ellis and watched her carefully when the judge placed the black cap on his head and pronounced the sentence of death.

She stood firm, erect, and unafraid.

It was then that I knew she had a heart of stone, that had once held premeditated murder; and that did not, even now, hold contrition.

Why should she escape the gallows? Jealousy is no motive for murder.

L. Webb
Casewick Road, West Norwood

5 July

Mrs Ruth Ellis's killing of David Blakely could not possibly have been manslaughter; if she had lied she could not have made it seem so. She loaded all six chambers of her gun and she fired them all. One bullet hit an unfortunate passer-by in the thumb; anyone might have been killed.

That Blakely was a lamentable specimen of humanity is neither here nor there. In England we quite rightly do not have degrees of murder. In America accused may plead guilty to second degree murder and in a few years a sentimental parole board lets him or her out once again.

In England every possible circumstance is taken into account by the Home Secretary and if, on his advice, the prerogative of mercy is granted the accused spends a long time in prison.

That is the English law and in my opinion it is the best law there is. It is true to say that untidy morally as the life was that Mrs Ellis led we do not hang people for immorality.

She had been unfaithful, even to Blakely, and it is difficult to understand why she should take his wish to leave her so seriously. But unpleasant as he was, he is dead, and the English are much too apt to forget the first corpse. True, Mrs Ellis told the truth, but truth, like patriotism, is not enough.

If the prerogative of mercy is granted, there is still no reason to minimise the seriousness of the crime, for that crime was murder.

(Miss) F. Tennyson Jesse,
Melina Place, St John's Wood

6 July

I say that Ruth Ellis should not hang. Of course she has offended against the law, but to hang a woman is to me a greater offence.

The argument of equality of the sexes is just tommy-rot. Women are different from men, in morals and behaviour. Men recognise this in their private relations with the opposite sex.

Judges are usually more lenient with women who commit offences than they are with male offenders. Why make a distinction for a capital offence?

Emanuel Shinwell
House of Commons

I have read with intense interest the letters in the *Evening Standard* concerning the case of Ruth Ellis. Who can now doubt that public opinion is far ahead of Parliament's stubborn adherence to the gallows?

But the issue is only confused when Raymond Chandler pleads for Ruth Ellis because she is a woman. Certainly the horror of hanging is increased when the victim is a woman but it is only a matter of degree.

My sympathy goes out to the padre muttering words of comfort to ears that cannot hear, to the hangman earning his livelihood by taking life, to the matron and the wardresses ensuring that nothing can happen to the woman until she reaches the end of her death walk.

My sympathy goes out to Lloyd George searching for some pretext to evade the law.

Finally my sympathy is with the community in whose name this legalised killing will take place. The human conscience is hammering at the prison gates. You can hear its voice in the public lobby of the Commons crying, 'Thou shalt not kill!'.

If this woman hangs, then the shame of it will be upon us all.

(Sir) Beverley Baxter,
House of Commons

7 July

In a number of murder cases there are circumstances which, though not in law justifying a verdict of justifiable homicide on the grounds of necessary self-defence or a verdict of manslaughter on the grounds of what amounts to provocation in law, or a verdict of not guilty by reason of insanity, do nevertheless convey to the ordinary reasonable mind a lessening of the accused's degree of moral guilt, justifying merciful consideration.

Thus, although a killing was not committed in circumstances of heat of blood which would justify reduction of the verdict to manslaughter by reason of provocation, the accused person may have been subjected, in fact, to a course of grievous and continuous provocation which would justify the exclusion of the death sentence. We are not informed whether or not there was any such circumstance in Ruth Ellis's case.

In the Union of South Africa, where I worked as a Supreme Court Judge for some 15 years, there is operating very satisfactorily a doctrine of extenuating circumstances, which enables all such accompanying facts of a case to be investigated.

The judge explains to the jury, or to the court in a non-jury trial, what, in the circumstances of the particular case, might amount to an extenuating circumstance. The jury or court then finds whether such an extenuation did, in fact, exist; and if this is affirmed, it is within the power of the judge to refrain from passing the death sentence and to impose some lesser penalty. This system enables the full facts of the case to be fully investigated.

(Hon.) C. W. H. Lansdown
(ex-Judge President of
the Eastern Districts Division of the
Supreme Court of South Africa),
Trafalgar Square, Westminster

We have read Miss Tennyson Jesse's letter referring to Ruth Ellis and David Blakely.

We notice she refers to him as 'a lamentable specimen of humanity'. Those of us, and there are many, who knew and loved David for years, wish to register our protest at these remarks.

We should require a great deal more proof than that provided by the defence at the trial that any of the allegations against his character were founded on fact.

(Mr and Mrs) Derek Blakely
[brother and sister-in-law of David Blakely],
Burgess Wood Road South, Beaconsfield

The tragic case of Ruth Ellis demolishes the common misconception that hanging is a deterrent. Ruth Ellis committed a murder quite deliberately, later refused to defend herself against the consequences, and still later refused to appeal. The threat of hanging had no deterrent effect at all.

The case of Frederick Cross, condemned to death at Staffordshire Assizes on Tuesday, is one in which the death penalty, far from being a deterrent, was a positive incentive to murder. 'I killed him so I would be hanged,' he told the police. And in court, against the judge's advice, he insisted on pleading 'Guilty.'

These two cases should bring nearer the abolition of this barbarous and immoral form of punishment.

Anthony Greenwood,
House of Commons

8 July

How many other women, I wonder, are going round now with a sense of deep shock in the back of their mind because Mrs Ellis, whom we never met, may be hanged on our behalf next week.

Certainly I am against all capital punishment because it seems to me only the lunatic killers—who live—are beyond understanding. But how can people behave smugly towards the Ruth Ellises of this world?

Their attitude reminds me of a man who, when I was doing a TV programme about road safety, said: 'No member of my family would ever dream of having an accident, only badly brought up people get hurt, and they should not be allowed out anyway.'

I am going to a party on the evening of the day Ruth Ellis is to hang. It seems almost indecent because if it were not for so many things that I can take no credit for, but only be grateful—such as a good education, varied interests, tolerant women friends—I might have committed her crime.

Any woman might have done so. Let's hope she will be reprieved to make a new life, and perhaps find some of the benefits most of us accept as our due.

Jeanne Heal,
Park Village West, St. Pancras

I applaud Miss F. Tennyson Jesse's letter. One cannot withhold compassion from Ruth Ellis, but if every woman poisoned by jealousy were allowed to take the law into her own hands without fear of the death penalty, then the position between the sexes would become untenable.

Love and hate may be concomitants, but murder is wholly incompatible with *real* love, while implicit in a violent and purely physical attraction from which this hysterical type of crime invariably springs.

In all this my thoughts are drawn to two poignant, stark figures who, so far, appear to have been forgotten—the parents of David Blakely. They have my heartfelt sympathy. Their suffering knows no reprieve.

Sonia Deane,
Park West, Paddington

9 July
There is a weak aspect of British law, not directly connected with justice, which the trial of Ruth Ellis once again exposes with some force. It is a matter which, as far as I know, has received but scant notice and concerns the length of time which legally has to elapse between trial, appeal if made, and date of execution of the condemned.

One is well aware that progress in legal matters is often slow but sure. It would appear unnecessary, however, to prolong to such an extent the interval between final legal arguments and the fulfilment of justice. Surely the Home Secretary should be capable of making up his mind in three days?

As at present legalised there is an interval of almost two weeks between the termination of all court proceedings and the execution of the murderer.

During this time, in cases of *cause célèbre* and particularly when a woman is concerned, public emotion on behalf of the condemned (often forgetting the dead victim) runs wild. This can do no good.

Quite apart from this, having decided that, legally, the law shall take its course, is there any reason to add to the death penalty the torture of waiting, day by day and hour by hour, the affixing of the noose?

(Dr) Nevil Leyton,
Harley Street, Marylebone

11 July
Don't let us turn Ruth Ellis into a national heroine. I stood petrified and watched her kill David Blakely in cold blood, even putting two further bullets into him as he lay bleeding to death on the ground.

What right had Ruth Ellis to be jealous of Blakely, jealous to the point of killing, even if there had been 'another woman'? She had another lover during the same period; that has been proved in evidence. What proof have we that the allegations against Blakely are true? He is dead and cannot defend himself. It is therefore distasteful and cruel to start a smear campaign against the boy to try to justify a dastardly murder.

Those hysterical people, getting up petitions for a reprieve, and those rushing to sign them. Do they realise Ruth Ellis shot Blakely to the danger of the public?

She might easily have killed me, an innocent passer-by, a complete stranger. As it is, I have a partly crippled right hand for life, for which there is no compensation.

If Ruth Ellis is reprieved, we may have other vindictive and jealous young women shooting their boy friends in public and probably innocent blood on their hands.

Crime passionel indeed! What if other countries would let her off from her just punishment. When has Britain followed the lead of others?

Let us remain a law-abiding country where citizens can live and walk abroad in peace and safety.

(Mrs) Gladys K. Yule,
Parliament Hill, Hampstead

How misconceived the letters of Sir Beverley Baxter and Mr Anthony Greenwood have been! Of course persons who actually commit murder have not been deterred by the threat of the death penalty. Similarly many lesser wrongdoers are not deterred by the threat of imprisonment—otherwise our prisons would be empty.

But who would ever suggest that the risk of prison was not a deterrent to many would-be wrongdoers who decide to refrain from crime?

No perfect deterrent against crime can be devised; otherwise crime could be abolished. But, to give only one instance, the risk of being hanged has surely caused many robbers and burglars to hesitate to allow one of their number to carry a lethal weapon the use of which might send them all to the gallows.

Abolish the death penalty and you risk the lives of policemen and innocent citizens.

(Sir) Ernest Goodman Roberts,
Ashley Gardens, Westminster

12 July

Ruth Ellis is to hang because she committed murder in the enlightened country of Great Britain.

Sergeant Emmett-Dunne has been found guilty of murder but, presumably, will not hang because his crime was committed in the unenlightened country of West Germany, which has done away with the death penalty.

Thus do we lag behind other peoples. We are steeped in a sodden savagery that is a shame to civilisation.

If Mr Lloyd George had reprieved Ruth Ellis, it would have meant the end of the hangman in this country. Faced with the dreadful decision, he reprieved the hangman, not the woman.

Those who believe in hanging might consider for a moment that the punishment will not end when the rope has efficiently severed the woman's soul from her body. Her two children will be haunted through the years, helpless and innocent.

Mr Lloyd George has, in effect, decreed that jealousy is not insanity. That may be the wisdom equal to that of Solomon. But there are many experts who take the opposite view.

Let us be logical and go back to the thumbscrew, the rack and the *auto-da-fé*. We have lost the right to speak for civilised society.

(Sir) Beverley Baxter,
House of Commons

APPENDIX 3

Leading article in *The Lancet*, 23 July 1955, and resultant correspondence

The Death Penalty

The laws against witchcraft were repealed in this country in 1736; but they had been recognised, long before that, as an ugly piece of inhumanity, disgracing the statute-book. To many of our countrymen today, and to whole peoples of some European countries, the death penalty seems as grotesque as did the witchcraft laws to 18th-century Englishmen. The feeling against it has been intensified by three notorious executions within the last few years: that of Evans, who may not have been guilty of the crime for which he was hanged; that of Bentley, who was not guilty of killing but of shouting—in a moment of violent agitation—incitement to another to kill; and that of Ruth Ellis, hanged for a murder done in a state of acute jealousy. All these people were executed in accordance with our country's law, after fair trial; but their deaths have excited a great deal of uneasiness, not only among those who, in an emotional frenzy, stood outside Holloway gaol on the eve of July 13, shouting 'Evans—Bentley—Ellis,' but among many whose sober concern it is that the laws of this country should be as worthy as any in the world, and among all who believe that an increasing preoccupation with murder trials and judicial executions is harming us as a people.

Capital punishment was abolished in New Zealand, Queensland, Denmark, Italy, the Netherlands, Norway, Sweden, and Switzerland, at dates ranging between 1870 and 1942; it remains legal in Belgium but (with one exception, in 1918) has not been enforced since 1863. Hence it is hardly surprising that the comment of other countries on the hanging of Mrs Ellis has been adverse and outspoken. To the Swedish people our failure either to abolish the death penalty or allow it to fall into disuse seems barbarous. To the French it seems that we apply it with a blind disregard of differences in the circumstances and character of the crime. Tried in other countries, some of the people we hang would suffer only a short term of imprisonment; and though we may condemn such leniency, we can hardly fail to be impressed by the very wide discrepancy in current punishments for identical offences.[1] Evidence received from Denmark, the Netherlands, Norway, and Sweden by the Royal Commission on Capital Punishment, 1949–53,[2] indicated that murderers who, after their release from imprisonment, commit further crimes of violence are rare, whereas those who become useful citizens are common. Figures published in the white-paper on Capital Punishment[3] show that the same is true of reprieved murderers in this country. Unlike some other crimes, murder is seldom part of a recognisable life-pattern: it appears unexpectedly, probably taking even the murderer by surprise. The habitual murderers —the Smiths and the Christies, obsessed by some emotional abnormality—are fortunately rare.

The opinions of foreigners on our practice might weigh little with us as a people were we ourselves entirely easy about it. But public protests against the executions of Bentley and Mrs Ellis make it quite clear that we are not. It has often been said, and is transparently true, that the death penalty punishes the innocent with the guilty. Not the criminal merely but his whole family, endure the alternations of hope

[1] A woman in Corsica, found guilty, at about the same time as Mrs Ellis, of the premeditated murder of a lover, was sentenced to two years' imprisonment and released at once on probation.

[2] Report of the Commission, p. 229. HM Stationery Office, 1953. See *Lancet*, 1953, ii, 713.

[3] Cmd. 7419.

and fear which a murder trial imposes—a long-drawn-out anguish far more horrible than all but the worst of murders. Once the sentence is carried out, the punishment of the criminal is complete—but not the punishment of his family, who have to live with the memory and stigma of his execution. Mrs Ellis leaves two young children, as well as her parents, to carry this unmerited burden. Such minorities deserve a voice. The children, who must inevitably be deprived of the 'normal home life' of which we nowadays speak so glibly, have been dealt, in addition, a most shattering psychological blow. Any law which, in its enforcement, does gross injury to innocent people strikes at the whole concept of justice.

And not these children only, but many others have been harmed by the recent emotional orgy. A father at Holloway Prison gates lifted up his six-year-old daughter so that she could say she had seen the notice announcing the death of Mrs Ellis. Children in a school near the prison are described by one of their teachers as being in a ferment: 'Some claim to have seen the execution from their windows, others spoke with fascinated horror of the technique of hanging a female.' Our means of communication are nowadays so efficient that the same unwholesome excitement was shared by children up and down the country. When an incident becomes the news of the day, presented at twenty million breakfast-tables, it becomes for the time an important part of our national life. The murderer, instead of quietly and decently receiving whatever deserts are deemed to be just, becomes the star of an immense and often long-remembered drama or even entertainment, quite frankly enjoyed by many people, and none the less because its horrors are true.

It is this aspect of the death-penalty which seems to us more dangerous and destructive than any other. As we said at the time of Bentley's hanging: 'Whether an execution is actually seen or imagined the mental effect is qualitatively the same, and in our view the perpetual preoccupation with the condemned cell and the gallows is harmful to the mental health of society.' We gild the worst of crimes with publicity, and associate it with an act of communal violence: small wonder if the youngsters swallowing the poison find the idea of violence dangerously attractive. Used as we use it, the death penalty may well be causing more crime than it prevents. Let us hope that those Members of Parliament who have launched a new attempt to get the law changed will succeed in freeing us from this recurrent demoralisation.

30 July

Sir,—*Indignor quandoque bonus dormitat Homerus!* There may conceivably be a rational case against capital punishment, but the highly emotive language of your leading article on the death penalty is quite unsuited to its presentation and does not in fact present it, being no more than an incoherent appeal to the emotions. That a collection of men and women already depraved in their tastes, and these further stimulated by a like-minded section of the press, should use the occasion of an execution for still more indulgence in debased behaviour outside a prison, is no more a ground against capital punishment than is the prevalence of shoplifting an argument against opening shops.

That we should seriously be invited to believe that the execution of Mrs Ellis deprived two children of a 'normal home life' is unworthy of your pages and no compliment to your readers' intelligence. The pattern of their lives may be glimpsed from the story of the squalid last weeks of their mother's life before she committed the crime for which she has paid the penalty. 'Normal home life' indeed! It may well be that now only does the possibility of this open before these children.

You go on to propose that 'any law which, in its enforcement, does gross injustice to innocent people strikes at the whole concept of justice.' What confusion of thought and what muddled ethics are here. It is apparently in vain that the enterprising editors of the Penguin Classics have made a translation of Aristotle's *Ethics* available for half a crown—less than the price of two copies of *The Lancet*.

It is not the law which is guilty of injustice to the innocent in this instance. It is the criminal herself who by her crime inflicts injustice upon her children, for it is her act that has made them suffer, and would have done so for the rest of their childhood even had her sentence been commuted to penal servitude. When a footpad robs with violence, is convicted and goes to prison for a long term, his innocent dependants—if he have any—suffer grave injustice in the form of distress, economic loss, the break-up of a family circle, and public humiliation. But is the law to be blamed for this injustice, and must the offender—as greatly against his family as against the State—go free and not to prison? In short, your article is, I must submit, barren of any rational concept of justice or appreciation of the rule of law.

Finally, I read that 'we gild the worst of crimes with publicity.' Who, pray, are 'we'? Surely no more than a cynical section of the press which, under the fiction of 'serving the public interest'—surely the most hypocritical fiction of our time—stirs up the mud and rakes the muck when sordid crimes such as the three you cite have been committed. If we were so fortunate as to enjoy a universally high-minded press, most of the objections—such as they are—that you urge against capital punishment, would vanish. But that we should be invited to abolish capital punishment because we have not got such a press (and this is the clear tenor of your argument) is a crazy proposition.

The injustice suffered by the innocent from the carrying out of the criminal law comes not from the law, but from the criminal himself and from those who for gain exploit his squalid life and crimes.

F. M. R. Walshe,
London, W1

Sir,—I think most people, and certainly most doctors, feel slightly sick when they read of, and visualise what actually happens at, an execution. The recent hanging of a young woman in the prime of her life was particularly nauseating. Is it not time that we doctors, the medical profession, unitedly denounced this senseless destruction of life for what it is: inhuman, barbaric, cruel, pointless and vindictive?

Deaths due to disease are tragedy enough; deaths due to accident are worse. But to think that we can deliberately and cold-bloodedly take it upon ourselves to authorise the death of a fellow human being is degrading and disgusting to the worst possible degree. There is also the ethical side of the matter. How can doctors, whether directly as prison medical officers, or indirectly as citizens in a democracy, have anything to do with the deliberate taking of human life? Our duty, our calling, is to prevent death and suffering and no other step can be condoned on any grounds whatsoever. I seriously question whether it is ethical for prison medical officers to assist in any way at an execution, to be present, to certify death, or to perform a post-mortem examination afterwards. If the authorities insist on carrying out this revolting undertaking, then they must do it alone, without the slightest help from us.

The public conscience has already been partly stirred. Unfortunately there are no half measures about death. Let us, as a profession, do all we can to induce the Government to think again, to go the whole way and abolish the whole filthy business once and for all.

W. Norman Taylor,
Geneva

Sir,—It is surprising that, so far as I know, no study of reactions to executions, using the techniques of Mass Observation, has been published. A great amount of material is available, and might include not only views expressed in the general press, but also from your own leading articles. As to the execution of Mrs Ellis, I doubt if you are right in saying that 'unwholesome excitement was shared by children up and down the country.' I have many opportunities of meeting children, at home and elsewhere, and I doubt their interest in the case. There are odd characters who may lift their children to read death notices, or take them to shows of relics of murderers; but this merely illustrates the well-known fact that there are odd people.

It is urgent that strong restraint be placed on press reports of crime.

In the Christie case, many doctors of long experience must have learned much that was new to them, both in physical pathology and in psychopathology. Surely it is unnecessary and undesirable to publish detailed evidence in such cases. For the expert these matters are to be found in technical works; for the ordinary man they have no value, and are indeed harmful. The law has already restricted the publication of certain evidence in divorce suits, and controlled 'horror-comics.' The breakfast-table is no place for a refresher course on the abnormal.

As to capital punishment in general, it may be that much of the debates that now precede, and follow, every execution arises from a misconception of the function of the courts.

Judges have often pointed out that the courts are courts of law, *not* courts of morals. The McNaughten rules are really based on moral theology, which assesses human acts on the bases of gravity of the act, knowledge of the agent, and volition of the agent. A man can reach no certain judgment on the absolute moral value of the act of another; his judgments are practical and inferential. A court makes a practical judgment as to whether the accused has broken an empirical code, which in general does, but not necessarily, correspond to moral standards. If we cease to regard the McNaughten rules as having a moral value, and cease to give to the courts a function, which they themselves disclaim, of making moral pronouncements, then the rules are seen as useful empirical standards, and the courts as the instruments of practical policies.

Capital punishment is not a penalty for a moral offence: it is a practical decision to remove permanently from the community a person who has made himself unsuitable to continue in it. The surgeon who excises a malignant focus makes no moral judgment on its cells; the battery commander who shells an unseen position does not judge the men holding it; the decisions are practical.

Again, we cannot really judge of the deterrent value of capital punishment. It may be that the execution of a Christie did assist some abnormal minds in achieving repression of certain tendencies; the knowledge of sanctions to be imposed may have a value even at the level of conditioned reflexes. It may be that the fact that the community does not accept sexual passion and jealousy as grounds for homicide has a value in maintaining for the whole community its background standards of conduct.

Finally it is to be hoped that some alternative to the present use of psychiatric evidence can be found.

It is far from edifying to the profession itself, and indeed to the lay public, to see that in most cases of homicide the defence can so often find evidence of psychic abnormality, the prosecution of 'normality.' 'Blackouts' have long been a jest among doctors: they are becoming a byword with the laity. It is odd that such evidence is so largely confined to charges of murder. Do forgers, adulterers of milk, and share-pushers not also suffer from these disorders?

I suggest the basic principle in considering punishment, and not only capital punishment, is that the courts are courts of law not courts of morals. In the matter of adultery we are content that the courts should enforce laws designed for the convenience and stability of the community, and not concern themselves with higher considerations of morality. Why not take the same view for murder?

R. C. Webster,
Todmorden, Lancashire

Sir,—If the death penalty is intended to protect the public, then surely no insane person should escape it if he commits a murder? Straffen will remain a potential threat to children until he dies, whereas Bentley, Mrs Cristofi, and Mrs Ellis would, had they been reprieved, quite possibly have harmed no-one afterwards.

Your leading article, which adduces strong arguments against the belief that hanging is a deterrent, may provide the Home Secretary with the evidence that there is a widespread feeling against capital punishment. What is to be feared is that, if this feeling continues to be ignored, juries will do as they did when hanging was the punishment for theft. They will refuse to convict.

W. A. Littlejohns,
London, SE12

Sir,—I should like to congratulate you on your leading article. Surely the term 'capital punishment' is an anachronism. In an enlightened age the chief object of punishment should be the correction and reform of the individual delinquent. It may be that the time is not yet ripe for the complete abolition of the death penalty; maybe the community is justified in ridding itself of a public menace; but having decided that such a measure is necessary the offender should be liquidated by the most humane method possible—which is certainly not hanging.

Among the most macabre features in the report of the Royal Commission were the details of the three weeks in the condemned cell. Surprisingly, the witnesses (including an eminent psychiatrist) appeared honestly to think that the procedure was humane. Physically the prisoner is well-treated—indeed no effort is spared to ensure that he is delivered to the executioner in good condition. All day and all night he (or she) is watched by two warders so that he has not a moment of privacy in which to think or pray, or to obey the calls of Nature. Surely reasonable precautions against suicide could be taken without this? Witnesses took pride in the fact that only about 90 sec. elapsed between the entry of the hangman and the drop. To effect this it seems that the scaffold is erected immediately adjacent to the condemned cell so that the victim sits for three weeks facing a wall which alone separates him from the gallows; he may also be aware of a peephole through which the hangman can watch him for technical details. By comparison, the ride to Tyburn seems humane, especially as in those brutal days most of the victims were fuddled with alcohol.

After the recent execution of Ruth Ellis, the pathologist who made the post-mortem examination thought it necessary to draw the attention of the coroner to the fact that there was a small quantity of brandy in the stomach. I had always hoped that prison medical officers contrived to arrange for condemned persons to be doped at the last. From the surprise expressed that somebody at Holloway Gaol had had the humanity to give Ruth Ellis a glass of brandy one fears that such hopes were without foundation.

T. W. Preston,
Horley, Surrey

Sir,—The ethical basis of capital punishment is, to say the very least, extremely shaky; but the ethics of prolonged imprisonment are far less often considered. As the law stands, the convicted murderer is condemned to death, but may be reprieved and then serve a life-sentence. When this happens those of us with vivid imaginations and more or less kind hearts do not find our breakfasts spoiled by the thought of the hideous paraphernalia of hanging; and, being made as we are, the thought of the horror of long imprisonment is soon forgotten. In the most recent case, there is no doubt that many people would have been much happier if the murderess had not been hanged;

but how would she have fared during years of prison? Prisoners are still human; and it is surely the duty of penologists to find some means of avoiding the degradation that is an ineluctable part of long imprisonment.

The 'shattering psychological blow' to the children would be almost equally great if they had to remember that their mother was in prison for murder. It is a charming idea that 'Any law which, in its enforcement, does gross injury to innocent people strikes at the whole concept of justice'; but even in Erewhon and Utopia the same thing happened.

A. Piney,
London, W1

6 August

Sir,—I write to assure Sir Francis Walshe, whose letter you published last week, that there is a rational case against capital punishment, but that the premises are not necessarily those which would be approved by Aristotle.

1. The destruction of one member of society by the rest, after due ceremony and deliberation, constitutes a suspension of an ethic which those very members of society are trying to uphold.

2. Can this be said to strengthen the ethic? Can this promote its establishment in Society?

3. Ethic is not given to us from some hypothetical source, nor does it grow on trees, nor in philosophical systems. It is slowly built up in society by the *ethical* activities of society. It is continually being suspended by individuals for their own purposes, and for this they are frequently punished.

4. Punishment is generally successful when conducted within the framework of the ethic—deprivation (robbery) punished by deprivation of that extension of property we recognise as 'liberty.' But when it is conducted in defiance of the ethic, there is a generally depressing effect upon the ethical activity of society.

5. To return to (1). When punishment involves the suspension of the ethic—that is, of the sanctity and preservation of human life, without which there is no ethic—society is mutilating itself twice over: once for the crime of the murderer, in which society plays its part unseen in the early years of the murderer; and again for its own crime of murdering the murderer, where it conducts the crime in full view of itself, with every possible histrionic aid, as a terrible warning to itself.

The second, more terrible, mutilation, is not necessary. It is *not* rational: it is barbaric.

J. J. Hamilton,
Brailsford, Derbyshire

Sir,—Surely the central point about the question of the death penalty is whether it deters from murdering. All responsible people feel that it would deter them, especially perhaps Home Secretaries, judges, policemen, and others who have the public safety in their charge. But that gives rise to a fallacy; such are the highly emotional circumstances in which murders are committed and so obsessed are the minds of murderers that it is doubtful whether this natural fear ever operates in deterrence. The Howard League, I recall, produced a mass of evidence showing how in those countries which had abolished capital punishment there had been no increase in the amount of capital crime—which is what one would expect—and I suggest *The Lancet* would be adding another logical argument to its splendid emotional appeal if it brought these figures up to date. For unless the death penalty deters from murder there can be nothing valid to be said for this grisly, irreparable punishment which, repeated two or three times a month year after year, degrades us all.

C. G. Learoyd,
Beckley, Rye, Sussex

Sir,—The letter of Sir Francis Walshe will, I am sure, find whole-hearted support from a large body of our profession. My only regret is that this letter, couched as it is in such superb English, and with such compelling argument, has not been quoted, in extenso, in our daily press.

C. B. Heald,
Rural Rheumatism Centre,
Chipping Campden,
Gloucestershire

Sir,—Your leading article of July 23 will receive very widespread support in the medical profession. There are, however, some considerations of another kind which should be stated.

1. Beyond the bald statement that a murderer has been condemned to death there is not the slightest necessity for any publicity. The prevailing obsession with horror, blatantly employed to increase newspaper circulations, is far more immoral than a judicial hanging.

2. The words 'punishment' or 'penalty' should have no place in the

treatment of the criminal. A surgeon by operating does not 'punish' a patient who is suffering from a duodenal ulcer. In the vast majority of cases the criminal is impelled to commit his crime by unconscious forces outside his control. He is, therefore, capable of being treated and sometimes cured of his criminal tendencies.

3. The choice of treatment must depend upon the existence and state of development of a moral sense. Where this is immature, treatment may involve imprisonment (or even flogging, just as one smacks a child when it persists in some dangerous act). Where the criminal has no moral sense and is a true psychopath he should be regarded as human refuse, dangerous to society, and quietly and humanely dispatched.

It is human personality and not life itself which is of paramount importance, and, while we are right in fostering and developing the former, we are under no necessity of regarding the latter as sacrosanct.

E. R. Matthews,
Bath

Sir,—May I add one point to the many raised in the varied correspondence which has followed your comprehensive leader. Is it not possible that Ruth Ellis had suicidal urges and wanted to die? By the manner in which she gave her evidence at trial (in spite of her excellent legal advisers) she made it very difficult for the court to do anything other than find her guilty.

Another case has occurred recently (at Uttoxeter) in which, according to the press reports, the murderer's main objective in killing his perfectly innocent victim was to satisfy his own suicidal urges by judicial hanging. At trial, he insisted on pleading guilty, and his desire to die was granted by a benevolent State. Thus the death penalty, far from being a deterrent, may actually be an incentive to murder.

In Sweden, and some of the other countries whom we disgust, the suicide-rate is higher than here. Perhaps, without realising it, in our usual blundering way we are being more humane than our apparently better enlightened neighbours.

J. F. Wilde,
Manchester

Sir,—The language used for condemning an occasional judicial death penalty is so much stronger than that for condemning the daily slaughter of innocents on the roads.

F. D. Saner,
London, W1

13 August

Sir,—I am interested in Dr Hamilton's assurance in your issue of Aug. 6, with its exposition of his private notion of ethics.

Yet, whatever he may say, ethics is part of philosophy, a subject not included in the medical curriculum and one not to be understood without some study. It is indeed a complex problem that he solves to his own satisfaction in half a column of *The Lancet*: one that has occupied the minds of men of genius for over two thousand years.

However, I must repeat, though I burden your patience, that if there be a valid case against capital punishment, your correspondent does not state it, nor appear to understand in what it must consist.

For example, he writes: 'Ethic (*sic*) is not given us from some hypothetical source, nor does it grow on trees, nor in philosophic systems. It is slowly built up in society by the ethical activities of society.'

He does not define an 'ethical activity,' nor tell us how we may recognise it as such. It remains something undefined and of hypothetical source, and without definitions of his operative terms, his sentences are devoid of rational content, and mean precisely nothing.

If ethics, like Topsy, 'just growed,' when do the activities of Society become ethical, and how do we know that they are so? What qualities —at the critical time—make ethical what was not so before? Which came first, the hen or the egg, the activities or the ethics? Dr Hamilton has no answers to these questions. It has not occurred to him that any are called for.

In reason, ethics must consist in *principles* that are applicable to human behaviour in all circumstances, though the science itself is not responsible for applying them in practice. They are not principles derived from conduct, but principles that should inform it.

Dr Hamilton confuses what he believes to be the growth of 'ethical activities' in society with the principles that must precede and determine this growth.

If there be a case against capital punishment, it is a pity that none of your correspondents is willing to pay it the compliment of a lucid and logical statement: making it clear whether, and how far, he takes his stands on ethics, upon grounds of simple expediency, because his sensibilities are affronted by the behaviour of a section of press and public when an execution is pending, or upon all these grounds each in its specified degree.

Yet, it has to be conceded that the principles and language of ethics, in which any such case must be couched, are no part of the training or experience of the doctor. This may be why, like Everyman, when he meets something he dislikes he finds it easiest to blow off steam: persuading himself that he has made a contribution to the problem, whereas he has done no more than relieve his feelings, and detonated a number of explosive adjectives. Whether this be an 'ethical activity' I leave to Dr Hamilton to pronounce.

F. M. R. Walshe,
London, W1

Sir,—I have read with great interest the correspondence that followed your editorial on capital punishment—chiefly that having recourse to Aristotle's *Ethics*.

Aristotle's *Ethics* are undemocratic, based on inequality, and anchored to the idea that a few men are infallible sages, who can dictate what virtue should be. Any deviation from this is wrong and unethical. Those sages are the legislators whose duty it is to make the young acquire moral habits so that eventually they practise virtue without the compelling power of the law. If the pupils acquire bad habits by listening to the same legislators they must be punished so that 'justice' be satisfied.

However sensible Aristotle's teachings may have been, to the modern mind, to say the least, they are devoid of common sense. There is no benevolence in them: the sufferings of mankind are things to be discussed intellectually only and no man must take a passionate interest in another man's unhappiness. Aristotle never learnt from human experience; he is absolutely barren of emotional considerations, and the deepest aspects of moral life never crossed his mind. His *Ethics* are absolutely repugnant to modern free-thinking and democracy; and his reactions to human beings are not far related to those of the hardened post-mortem attendant and have nothing in common with the kind and sympathetic approach of the true doctor, whose main concern is the preservation of life.

No-one has better summed up the *Ethics* of Aristotle than that great contemporary philosopher Bertrand Russell: 'What he has to say is what will be useful to comfortable men of weak passions; but he has nothing to say to those who are possessed by a god or a devil, or whom outward misfortune drives to despair.'

L. R. Celestin,
Thames Ditton, Surrey

Sir,—It is difficult to discuss the death penalty unemotionally, but there would seem to be at least two points against its continuance which do not involve emotional considerations.

The result of a fair legal procedure, like the result of scientific work, can be expressed only as a probability. It would be as well, therefore, to inflict only such penalties as are reversible. Secondly, it has been shown that evidence as to the deterrent effect of capital punishment is equivocal. In other words, it is doubtful whether the ordinary citizen need feel that his already remote chance of being murdered would be increased were the death penalty abolished. The police are entitled to think differently about this matter, but perhaps the provision of very severe penalties against the unauthorised carrying of lethal weapons would provide them with a better safeguard.

T. D. Day,
Ilkley, Yorkshire

20 August

Sir,—Sir Francis Walshe takes you to task, in his letter of July 30, for using 'emotive language.' But if emotive language will help doing away with this butchery, let us have more and more of it. Major Lloyd-George has said that he will reconsider abolition when there is 'overwhelming public *sentiment*' in favour of such a step. If you, Sir, in your 'emotive' editorial, have contributed towards building up that sentiment, then you may well be satisfied.

In the same issue, Dr Webster salves his conscience by hiding behind the phrase 'courts are courts of law not courts of morals.' But that is precisely the terrible thing about British law. We are in the grip of a robot-like inhuman automaton. The button is pressed and the dial shows *death*. Instead of judges, might it not be better to substitute electronic brains? At least the judges would then be spared the 'ordeal' they often complain of. Surely, Sir, the law was made for man, not man for the law. And the law is supposed to be interpreted by human beings, not machines.

Dr Piney (July 30) also has a neat way of evading the issue, a way that does credit to us as a nation of horse and dog lovers. 'Put the poor creatures out of their misery,' he says in effect. No doubt he thinks it unfortunate that doctors have not quite the same powers as veterinary surgeons. It would be as logical to recommend that all animals serving life sentences in the zoo should be put to death, and, as a next step, euthanasia for everybody in Broadmoor. Actually, in the case of Ruth Ellis, it appears possible that she did welcome death and might have committed suicide if given the chance—and most of us hope that this mercifully was the case. But it is no excuse for us to aid and abet suicides by providing a qualified hangman for the purpose.

We cannot make excuses for death under any guise. Do not let us try.

W. Norman Taylor,
Geneva

Sir,—No-one is more appreciated for the accuracy of his aim and the penetrating power of his criticism than Sir Francis Walshe, but he was sadly off form in his letter of July 30. How could he say that you invited us to believe that Mrs Ellis's execution deprived her children of normal home life when you clearly wrote: 'The children, who must inevitably be deprived of the "normal home life" of which we nowadays speak so glibly, have been dealt, in addition, a most shattering psychological blow.'

Surely he can see that it is devastating for a child to grow up with the knowledge that Society, Authority, the State, call it what you will, after careful deliberation, decided to kill his mother? I agree with the Editor of *The Observer* who told his readers that each one of them shared the responsibility for these hangings, and I feel, Sir, that you should have told your readers that their responsibility is 1000 times that of the general public. For of the three professions directly concerned in judicial hanging, the Church seems indifferent, the bishops being content to leave the delicate duty of reconciling the teachings of Christ with their blessing on the hangman's labour to the prison chaplains; and the Law as always places legality before justice. Medicine alone offers hope.

For not only have we the public's ear on every aspect of behaviour but no man can be hanged unless a doctor explicitly or implicitly certifies him sane. And none of us can be compelled to give our opinion unless we choose to do so.

The extraordinary thing about this correspondence is that Sir Francis appears to put himself on the hangman's side. Yet, one needs to have come no nearer than the back row of one of his clinical demonstrations to know that he is a physician of the greatest understanding and humanity. It is impossible to imagine him having the care of a condemned man and then, on the appointed day, handing him over to the executioner.

The reason for the persistence of this barbarous practice lies, I suggest, in overspecialisation which has reduced each individual's responsibility to a tolerable fraction. The prosecutor, juryman, judge, doctor, and hangman each does his part, though none surely could be found willing to do the whole.

We can most easily break the chain: therefore our responsibility is the greatest.

J. F. Tuthill,
Droitwich

Sir,—Sir Francis Walshe is severely critical of those who oppose capital punishment and he accuses them of emotionalism, but one searches in vain for a single rational argument to justify capital punishment in his two letters.

All moral systems include some such principle as 'Thou shalt not kill.' However, in the past, governments have found it 'expedient' to make exceptions under certain circumstances. For instance, in war-time we are instructed to murder our fellow creatures in as large numbers as possible. When there is a revolution, the government considers it highly moral to annihilate the 'rebels.' (Of course, the rebels consider this highly immoral.) If a citizen commits a murder, the State does not consider it immoral to murder him by hanging —presumably on the primitive principle of 'eye for eye' and 'tooth for tooth.' The latest demand for more sanctions to murder comes from the euthanasia enthusiasts, who would have us kill human beings with their consent (e.g., cancer sufferers, and psychotics who express suicidal desires), and also without their consent (e.g., imbeciles, idiots, and dements). The ethical question is, should there be any exceptions to the Sixth Commandment? It does not require a meticulous study of the history of philosophy during the past two thousand years to give an answer, as Sir Francis Walshe would seem to imply. The answer should obviously be in the negative, and it is indeed a terrible indictment of our low level of ethical development that we should still be debating this question.

I. Atkin,
Park Prewett Hospital, Basingstoke

3 September

Sir,—With the greatest respect to some of your correspondents, I think that they are making this matter too complicated. Ethical problems may indeed have been occupying the minds of men of genius for over two thousand years; yet it is a strange fact that most great ethical advances, such as the abolition of slavery, have not, I think, arisen out of brilliant, logical, and lucid expositions of the philosophers. One of the great failings of our generation is the deification of the intellect; yet as Christians—and we are a Christian country—we know that wisdom is granted to quite simple people, unversed in the language of philosophy, where matters of right and wrong are concerned.

This may be dubbed as mere emotional thought; but many of us believe that the death penalty, like war, is neither effective in its object nor in line with our interpretation of the Christian way of life. To such simpler folk this is sufficient answer to the problem.

Paul Hickinbotham,
Leicester

Sir,—Sir Francis Walshe (Aug. 13) asks for the rational argument against capital punishment. May I quote it, *sans m'engager*?

The object of the death penalty is primarily to deter potential murderers. In some countries and in parts of countries the penalty has been abolished or temporarily suspended. In these circumstances neither the rate nor the trend of the rate of murder has been significantly changed.

If these propositions are correct, then capital punishment fails in its main object, and, unless there are other arguments for maintaining it, it should be abolished.

C. W. M. Whitty,
Oxford

Sir,—I am what James Thurber would describe as a man with big brown eyes and a tiny mind; and so discussion on ethics, Aristotle, and philosophy is well above my head.

In theory I may support abolition of capital punishment, but, as a father of small children, in the event of their murder I should naturally desire revenge. Hatred is as natural a feeling as love.

The important point that has so far been missed is that the final responsibility for the continuance of the death penalty rests upon the electorate. If people want murderers to be hanged, they will be. If they desire the penalty to be changed, they must mandate their representatives accordingly.

Dr Day's letter of Aug. 13 calls for comment. He suggests severe penalties for the unauthorised carrying of lethal weapons. But how many murders are committed by lethal weapons (and I take it Dr Day means guns, knives, and coshes)? Surely the common methods of murder are hammers, axes, carving-knives, and last, but by no means least, a pair of hands. Are these everyday articles to be outlawed?

On the morning that Ruth Ellis died I realised she was paying the penalty for a cold-blooded murder: and yet when I looked at my watch at 9.15 A.M. I felt a little sick. But not as sick as the day the Rosenbergs were electrocuted.

Hanging may be right or wrong, I just don't know. But from a practical point of view, it is the public that must decide to retain the rope, or find another method of coping with this particular crime.

F. E. D. Griffiths,
Kenilworth

Sir,—Sir Francis Walshe asks for a 'lucid and logical statement' in support of the case against capital punishment. I wonder whether he regards this as a logical statement: to take deliberately somebody's life is today regarded as the most abominable crime man can commit. (I do not know whether there are any 'logical' reasons for this general conviction or whether it is a purely 'emotional' attitude.) How then can we, in spite of our severe condemnation of deliberate killing, empower and pay a person to do just this?

I know society allows—and may even order—men to kill in self-protection, but only in cases of utter emergency. A handcuffed prisoner does not confront us with such an emergency. The potential danger which he may still represent can effectively be dealt with without anybody having to commit the crime which everybody professes most deeply to abhor. May this abhorrence be founded on a logical or psychological basis, the abolition of the death penalty must be the logical consequence of this generally professed abhorrence.

Lise Gellner,
St Lawrence's Hospital,
Caterham, Surrey

Sir,—Sir Francis Walshe says that it is a pity that none of your correspondents make a 'lucid and logical statement' against capital punishment. But surely no-one, least of all a doctor, needs to find elaborate excuses to save a life. On the contrary, the onus lies on those who wish to see their fellow humans put to death to find a *very* good reason why it should be done.

W. Norman Taylor,
Geneva

10 September

Sir,—Is Dr Whitty right? The primary objects of the death penalty are (1) to punish the criminal; and (2) to prevent the culprit from repeating the offence. Whether capital punishment acts as a deterrent is secondary and open to discussion. Statistics do not seem to help. Common sense suggests that it might.

Harold Kisch,
London, W1

APPENDIX 4

In January 1956 a survey of public opinion regarding capital punishment was carried out by Mass-Observation (UK) Ltd for the *Daily Telegraph*. Of the stratified sample of 6,110 persons, approximately 1,000 said that they had recently heard, seen or read something that helped them to make up their mind on the issue.

	Those approving capital punishment (per cent)	*Those disapproving (per cent)*
Ellis murder case	8	24
Bentley-Craig case	2	9
Evans-Christie case	1	9
Other named murder cases	4	3
Other unnamed murder cases	21	10
Murder cases of any description	38	43
A general increase in crime	8	–
Dangers to children and old people	19	2
Miscarriages of justice	–	12
Activities of 'Teddy boys'	3	–
Effect on those who are left	–	1
Miscellaneous answers	6	9
Number of cases	670	328